HOW TO TEACH MATH TO BLACK STUDENTS

*By Shahid Muhammad
"The Math Doctor"*

African American Images
Chicago, Illinois

TABLE OF CONTENTS

PREFACE

The inspiration and motivation to write this book evolved from years of interaction with Black students, many of whom were deficient in basic skills, slow in comprehension, and lacking in confidence and interest. Although these students possessed differences in educational backgrounds and learning styles, I noticed that most of them had one thing in common -- a dislike and fear of mathematics.

Through interaction with these students, I came to realize that most, if not all of the deficiencies and negative attitudes were due to the influence of previous mathematics teachers, who had neither the proper knowledge nor the correct approach to teach these children. Therefore, many of the children came to my class with preconceived notions about mathematics, low self-esteem and self-worth, and extreme deficiencies in computational, analytical, and problem-solving skills. My desire is to transform the current status of Black students performance in mathematics. Therefore, in this book I offer teaching methods, strategies, and methodologies that not only worked for me but have shown almost miraculous results. After implementing these strategies and teaching methods in your classroom, you will begin to notice a transformation taking place in the students mathematical aptitude and performance. You will also notice a tremendous increase in their interest and a change in attitude toward mathematics and learning in general.

Although these strategies and methodologies are specifically designed for the Black student, you will find that this book provides assistance and guidance for the mathematics education of all students, regardless of race, age, or religious background. I believe this book can be a torchlight for the entire educational system and can only aid in rescuing our students from the current mathematical illiteracy that exists in American society as a whole and among Black students specifically.

I hope that the contents of this book will be utilized by those who care about the mathematical competence of our children and our society. We are living in a country where mathematical literacy and competency ranks far below many of the less-developed nations. If we are to produce a future generation that can keep up and compete with the technological and scientific minds of other nations, it is incumbent upon us to develop new and improved methods of mathematics education. This book is just one step toward that goal.

CHAPTER ONE:
SELF AND MATHEMATICS

We all know that when a friend or a relative informs us that they have some pictures for us to look at, the first question on our mind is, "Am I in the pictures?" This is the same question that Black students are silently asking themselves each time they enter a classroom to partake in the learning process.

There are hardly any mathematics textbooks or curricula that inculcate the images and contributions that Blacks have made to mathematics. This serious error is one of the main stumbling blocks to building self-esteem and self-confidence in Black students in the mathematics classroom. Because of the negative and destructive pictures that society paints of Black people, Black students have a very bleak and dismal perception of their academic abilities. Since Black students do not find themselves in the mathematics curriculum nor in the sphere of mathematics as a whole, they develop an "I can't do it," "This is not for me," "Who cares?" attitude.

In order to stop this destructive pattern and cycle, the true history of mathematics as it pertains to Blacks must be presented and taught as a foundation. Teachers must teach the students about the great Black mathematicians and scientists of the past and present. Black students should be made aware that the first mathematicians were Black and that Black people in the past had developed mathematics to such a high degree that many scholars and scientists even today marvel at the civilizations and architecture they built.

In most mathematics textbooks used in this country, Black mathematicians are rarely, if ever, mentioned. Textbooks and teachers must inform students that most of the great White mathematicians of the past received their education and knowledge from Egyptian schools and temples. Greats such as Euclid, Pythagoras, and Aristotle all studied under or were inspired by Egyptian scholars and priests. It is crucial for the teacher to inform and illustrate to students that the Egyptian people were Black just like them.

In order to inspire and motivate Black students toward mastery in mathematics, a thorough knowledge of self as it pertains to mathematics is absolutely necessary. If the teacher is not equipped with proper and correct knowledge of the role of Black people and their contributions in the field of mathematics, then it is incumbent upon them to do the research necessary to properly prepare themselves.

Perception of ones ability is directly related to one's academic performance. Since society has distorted and clouded Black students perceptions to the point that they cannot visualize Black people excelling in and mastering mathematics, they are comfortable and satisfied with achieving at a below-average or average level in the mathematics classroom.

In order to change this situation, teachers must combine the students reality and history with the mathematics curriculum and instruction. We must connect each student as an individual to the mathematics content and material. The student must be able to see himself or herself in the educational process and in the overall picture. Here are a few methods and strategies that can be used to accomplish this task.

INTERGRATING BLACK CONTRIBUTIONS TO MATHEMATICS

Teachers can integrate the contributions made by Blacks to science, technology, and mathematics into their lesson plans and activities. This can be done by designing activities or research around these individuals or simply mentioning them and the role mathematics has played in their lives. Here are just a few examples of famous Blacks that could be mentioned and studied in the math class: 1) Imhotep, 2) Al Khwarizmi, 3) Charles Drew, 4) George Washington Carver, 5) Lonnie Shabazz, 6) Mae Jemison, 7) Benjamin Banneker, 8) Jan Ernst Matzeliger, 9) Daniel Hale Williams, 10) Garret A. Morgan, 11) Frederick Mckinley Jones.

Teachers should also heavily stress how each of these greats used mathematics in their respective field and career.

Because most of the mathematics textbooks make little or no mention of the contributions of Blacks to mathematics, teachers should teach a true historical account of how the science of mathematics had its origin and roots in Africa. Black students would be highly inspired and motivated to know that the Egyptian people built the Pyramids, the Sphinx, and many other outstanding architectural structures.

Lessons and activities can also be centered around the great Black role models and heroes of today. The teacher can demonstrate to the students how some of the famous Black entertainers, politicians, educators, scholars, and scientists of today utilize mathematics in their fields of endeavor. Students can do research assignments, conduct interviews, or do projects using the information they receive. This will help them realize that Black people can master mathematics and that mathematics is prevalent in almost all careers and professions.

TEACHING THE UNIVERSALITY OF MATHEMATICS

Mathematics is not a separate science, isolated and irrelevant to the world in which we live. Mathematics can be found in every aspect of life and throughout this vast universe. However, because Black students rarely see any positive role models involved in the study of mathematics, they possess a false perception that mathematics is irrelevant to their reality or that Blacks are not competent enough to become mathematically literate.

SELF AND MATHEMATICS

This is why teachers must illustrate and demonstrate how mathematics is at the root of everything in existence as well as an integral part of the lives of Black people. Teachers can start with the individual student and demonstrate how each student is mathematical. Mathematics can help explain the human body, which is composed of chemicals that occur in particular percentages. The body, just like the earth, is 75 percent water. Teachers can associate the concept of functions and relationships to those between the weight and height of a person. The student's heart rate, pulse beat, length and width of intestines, and weight of their brain, are just a few areas where teachers can help students see how mathematics plays a major role in their lives as individuals. Such insights will allow students to see that learning mathematics means: I am learning about myself. Each time the student masters a concept in mathematics, they master a part of themselves.

Not only are Black students preoccupied with themselves but they are also fascinated by sports and entertainment figures whom they look up to for guidance and inspiration. Many of the students become so fascinated by these individuals that they care more about the individual's life than they do their own. An excellent way to turn this into positive energy for the math class is to use the sports figures and entertainment stars to demonstrate and illustrate how mathematics plays a key and crucial role in their everyday lives and activities.

Imagine the inspiration and enthusiasm students would have toward mathematics if they found out that Michael

HOW TO TEACH MATH TO BLACK STUDENTS

Jordan uses mathematics to shoot the ball and glide through the air, that their favorite music artists use mathematics to make records, or that the video games they love to play require the use of mathematics. Teachers can create lesson plans around the use of mathematics in each of these fields. This will create a greater and deeper appreciation for mathematics and will inspire the students toward mastery of the subject.

Another way to demonstrate to students the universality of mathematics is to connect their interests, hobbies, and daily activities to mathematics. Teachers can have students fill out surveys indicating their hobbies, interests, clubs, and activities. Once this is completed, the teacher can develop lessons and activities that integrate students interests with mathematics. For example, most students like sports. Many mathematical concepts and skills are utilized in sports. In basketball, there are free-throw percentages to calculate, and in baseball, batting averages.

If the students are interested in model rockets, the teacher may do a lesson on altitude or velocity. If students are interested in computer games, the teacher may do a lesson on flow-charting or functions. Many Black students are interested in keeping up with the latest fashions and designs. The teacher can channel this interest by teaching a lesson on similarity, which is important in designing and making clothes. There are many examples and applications that teachers can use to integrate students interests and hobbies with mathematics.

SELF AND MATHEMATICS

Once students see the relevancy of mathematics then they will become more attentive to the lesson material and will retain more information, since they are making a mental connection to something they like. This will also create a desire in students to learn mathematics, since they can see themselves in the big picture. When students realize that mathematics plays an integral role and a crucial part in their lives as individuals, they become more enthusiastic and are stimulated to learn as much as they can about it.

We as educators must get in tune with the needs, aspirations and desires of the students. Each individual student has his or her own needs, wants, likes, and dislikes. The more we can tap into the sphere of the students world and incorporate mathematics into their thinking, the greater success we will have in motivating, inspiring, and encouraging them to excel and master mathematics.

CHAPTER TWO:
CHANGING OUR FOCUS

There are so many problems with the American educational system that one could become befuddled and tired attempting to list and find solutions for all of them. However, one major problem that must be faced and resolved if we desire to prepare our students for the future, is to develop their critical thinking skills.

In most schools, students, particularly Black students, are neither taught how to think nor are they really required to utilize the power of their minds. There is a serious void in the mathematics classroom when it comes to teaching critical thinking, reasoning, and analyzing skills. Educators are producing robots as opposed to thinkers. We are producing computation-centered versus concept-centered students.

Today's student is bombarded with various stimuli that require little or no thinking or reasoning skills. Youth occupy most of their free time watching television, listening to music, playing sports and games, or eating. This has created a serious problem in our society that has placed the mathematical performance and literacy of our students far below the national averages of many less-developed countries. It behooves us, as mathematics teachers, to turn this situation around by providing education that cultivates, nourishes, and stimulates critical thinking and reasoning skills. We must eliminate the robotic or calculator mentality and work to produce thinkers, analyzers and problem solvers.

How are we producing a robotic or calculator mentality? Consider the calculator. It is simply a machine that performs mathematical operations rapidly. Likewise, a robot only performs the orders and instructions that are programmed into its memory banks. The robot and calculator do not think or reason for themselves; they simply produce answers. Such answers are produced quickly and accurately but are void of meaning and significance, if they are not applied to some real-world problem.

This is exactly the focus and aim of most mathematical classrooms across the country. Teachers are concerned only with how accurately and how rapidly students can compute arithmetic operations, simplify algebraic expressions, solve algebraic and trigonometric equations, find the derivative of a function or integrate an expression. We are turning our students into calculators and robots. We give them 50 to 100 problems to solve based on the same skill, principle, or concept. The aptitude of a student is measured by how well he or she can imitate the algorithms or procedures utilized by the instructor or by how well he or she can regurgitate rules, theorems, postulates, and formulas that are void of practicality or relevancy.

Mathematics is a pure and exact science that is capable of solving real problems. Educators and students must understand that without the problem-solving and applications aspects of mathematics, it becomes vague, irrelevant, and useless. Teaching mathematics for the sole purpose of producing meaningless answers and solutions is like teaching a person about a hammer, but never showing them how to use it.

Those involved in teaching mathematics must change the focus and aim of mathematics education. We must begin to instill critical thinking, reasoning, and analysis skills into the children so they can receive the full benefit of studying and mastering mathematics. How can this be done? What methodology is needed to accomplish this? Here are a few methods and strategies that can be used.

I. Provide Higher Levels of Questioning

The tasks and duties that students are required to perform in the mathematics classroom mainly exhibit one level of questioning. There are many different levels of questioning that require the student to increase their understanding of and ability to apply concepts and skills. The higher the level of questioning, the deeper the understanding and comprehension.

Questioning is a very vital component of mathematics education. For it is by questioning our students that we receive feedback and data on their level of mastery and retention of the material they have been exposed to. Unfortunately, most mathematics teachers relegate their entire range of questioning to one level, which is usually the lowest. Yet, it is the level of questioning that distinguishes a robot from a thinker. When students are trapped at the lowest level of questioning, they are simply regurgitating information, algorithms or formulas, but memorizing does not necessarily mean that critical thinking or reasoning has taken place.

The lowest level of questioning, Level 1, involves simple memory skills. At this level students are required to memorize rules, postulates, theorems, algorithms, definitions, and properties. Then teachers design activities, assignments, quizzes, and exams based upon how accurately and efficiently students can extrapolate and recite the information. Questions at this level are of the type that would be found on a multiple-choice, true-false, or completion exam. These types of exams serve a significant purpose, but they cannot be the entire focus and single tool used for evaluating a student.

When knowledge has truly been understood and comprehended, it must take the form of application. Knowledge alone is dead without the application of that knowledge. This applies to learning mathematics. If a student can only memorize and recite information, but cannot analyze, problem solve, experiment, or synthesize on the basis of that information, then that student does not have a true mastery or understanding of it and is limiting the power of his or her mind. This is the dilemma that we find most students in when we look at the tasks and duties given to them by their math teachers.

Students are not cultivating their thinking skills because they are not being required to go beyond the first level of questioning. Students are given assignments that require minimal critical thinking, reasoning, and problem-solving skills. For example, most students are given assignments that involve solving or simplifying 30 to 50 problems, all of which require the same skill, rule, or concept. Students are given worksheet upon worksheet of problems that have no meaning, relevance, or application in terms of any real problem. Students are given true-false exams and multiple-choice questions, which require the student only to remember the minimum amount of information needed to perform well enough to pass the test. The need for lessons designed around higher levels of questioning is obvious.

Lets look at how we as teachers can take a simple task or problem at Level 1 and design questions and tasks at higher levels. Here are some practical ways and methods of questioning at progressively higher levels.

At the elementary level, you may have the students do the following:

Level 1——Solve this problem:
$$5 + 10 = ?$$
Level 2——How can you show what $5 + 10$ is equal to?
Level 3——Is this problem correct? Why or why not?
$$5 + 10 = 17$$

> Level 4——What is the difference between 5 + 10 and 10 + 5?
>
> Level 5——John bought 8 apples, 6 pears and 3 plums at the produce market. How many pieces of fruit did he buy altogether?
>
> Level 6——Write a report on how the ancient Egyptians used the skill of addition.

Notice how we started with a simple addition problem and expanded the level of questioning. This type of progression from stage to stage of questioning, stimulates thinking and reasoning skills as well as evaluates the students true understanding and mastery of the relevant concepts and skills. Notice that as the level of questioning increases in difficulty, the degree of thinking needed also increases. The questions also broaden the students scope and perception of mathematical concepts and skills, thereby giving them a greater appreciation for mathematics and the learning process as a whole.

Teachers can utilize the different levels of questioning as a wonderful and innovative way to evaluate each students performance and mastery of lesson objectives. The students who score high at the lower levels of questioning should be looked upon as students who require a little more teaching and instruction. Students who perform well at the higher levels of questioning are the most advanced and above-average learners. To evaluate all levels; assignments, quizzes, and exams should include questions at each level to provide an adequate assessment of each student's ability.

Here are some examples on the secondary level:

Level 1——Solve this inequality:

$$X + 5 > 3$$

Level 2——What does x<-2 mean?

Level 3——Is 2 a solution to x + 5>3? Why or why not?

Level 4——What is the difference between x + 5>3 and X + 5>-3? What are the similarities?

Level 5——James wants to go to the movies but he is not sure whether he has enough money. Movies cost $6.00. He will also need money to buy some snacks to eat during the movie. If James does not want to spend more than $11.00, what is the most he can spend for snacks?

Level 6——Write a report on the history of the inequality symbols.

II. The Why and When of Conceptualization

One way to develop thinkers as opposed to robots is to instill in students the why and when of every mathematical concept, procedure, skill, and rule. Most students can imitate what the teacher does and how the teacher applies a rule, but how many can explain why the principle, concept, or rule works.

HOW TO TEACH MATH TO BLACK STUDENTS

We must instruct the student in a manner that reveals the relevance and validity of every mathematical rule, law, or skill to make sure it is clearly defined and understood. Students must not only know the information but be able to articulate why it works the way it does and be able to prove it. This will provide the student with a deeper understanding of and greater appreciation for mathematics.

One of the greatest and most pertinent questions that can be asked is why. Students are neither comfortable nor satisfied with learning an enormous array of facts, theorems, rules, and shortcuts that are void of rationale, usefulness, and proof. When students can comprehend facts and rules— and also verify and apply them—they begin to use their thinking and analyzing skills, which, as we have already discussed, is desperately missing from the math classroom.

For example, if students are learning how to subtract fractions using regrouping or renaming, it is not enough just to provide examples and guidance on how the skill is executed. But it is much more meaningful to teach students why the skill works and why it is used. Think how wonderful it would be if students could prove that renaming or regrouping is a valid method for solving subtraction of fractions problems. When students can explain, verify, rationalize, and prove, they are nourishing and exercising their minds. We all know that in order to build muscles, pressure and stress must be placed on them. It is the same with the students minds. Teaching them the why and when of conceptualization places pressure on their minds and builds their thinking skills.

We must also instruct students on when to use a rule, skill, or law in mathematics. Many students learn basic arithmetic operations but without learning when to use them, they cannot solve real-world problems or applications involving them. For example, when we teach students how to divide, most teachers give them examples and demonstrate how the operation is executed. Then they give the students similar problems to do for homework or class work. However, if those same students were asked to determine how many cartons of 12 would be filled with 55 apples, many would be totally bewildered and perplexed. The reason is that the students were not taught what division is all about. They were not instructed on the true definition and meaning of division. They were only given examples on how to, but never instructed or guided on why or when. Students must know when to use division in order to grasp the true essence of the mathematical concept.

If Black students were instructed in this manner, they would not be turned off by mathematics because they think it is too vague, abstract, or irrelevant to their reality. By teaching them the why and when, they gain confidence in themselves and in the curriculum, and their performance will escalate toward excellence.

Black students will also benefit from this focus in the area of retention. One of the most prevalent problems I have noticed among students is their inability to retain information and knowledge. This is where teaching the why and when of concepts aids greatly. When students gain a thorough, root knowledge of concepts, it is easier for them to retain mathematical knowledge because they understand the principle of that knowledge, and principles can be applied in various situations. The same mathematical principles and properties continuously reappear in many different branches of mathematics. Therefore, if students grasp the why and when of concepts, they can solve any number of mathematical problems or situations since the principles and properties are constant.

Another benefit of this method is that it strengthens the students foundation, which provides a springboard and base upon which other, more complex, and higher-level concepts, principles, and skills can be built. Mathematics is an interlocking and integrated science. Each concept and skill builds on the previous skill. Therefore, if students gain a firm and stable hold on the basic concepts through learning the whys and whens, they will enjoy a smooth transition from stage to stage on their journey through the world of mathematics.

III. Games, Puzzles, and Brain Teasers

An excellent method of fostering critical thinking and reasoning skills, while creating a learning environment bubbling with fun and excitement, is to introduce games and puzzles into the instructional activities. I have found this to be an excellent source of motivation and inspiration in my classroom throughout the years. You cannot imagine the level of excitement and enthusiasm that is created when students are involved in competitive activities or when they are pondering over the solutions to puzzles and brain teasers. These simple additions bring excitement to the entire classroom. Because Black students are already preoccupied with sport and play, integrating competitive games and activities into the math curriculum allows learning to take place with the same energy and vigor that students exert when they are involved in sport and play. Students become caught up with the fun and excitement of the games, and they forget that they do not like math or that math is too difficult. You will find that some of your slower students will rise to the occasion and put forth greater effort just so they can win the game at hand.

Black students have a short attention span when it comes to expository learning. Teachers cannot simply lecture students and expect them to be motivated and interested in the subject matter. This is why the implementation of mathematical games is an excellent method for keeping students interested and attentive. Since they love to use their energy for sport and play, why not channel that same energy toward the goal of mastering mathematics.

The use of brainteasers and mathematical puzzles is usually relegated to the more advanced or gifted students, because most teachers believe that these students are the only ones capable of solving them. However, I have found that using brainteasers and puzzles in the classroom not only inspires and excites the gifted and above-average student but also creates stimulation and motivation in the slower student. Students in general, whether they are slow or advanced, get wonderful satisfaction from challenging their minds with puzzles and brainteasers. It is not that they always have to get the right answer or solve the puzzle; they get great satisfaction from just attempting. The difficulty of the brainteaser or puzzle provides satisfaction and enthusiasm for the students. It is similar to playing basketball. Everyone loves to make a lay-up, but students get more gratification and enjoyment out of trying the most difficult shot. The greater the difficulty and the more pressure placed on their minds, the greater the satisfaction and pleasure.

Using brainteasers and puzzles in the mathematics class provides development in many areas of the mind that must be invoked to advance to higher, more complex sciences and mathematics. Some areas that can be enhanced and developed are critical thinking skills, reasoning abilities, visualization and perception skills, and problem solving and deduction. The more you expose students to puzzles and brain teasers, the more their minds grow, until they hatch creative thoughts and ideas that may have lain dormant in the student's mind. It is through the mind of our children that solutions and remedies to our problems will emanate. Therefore, it is incumbent upon us to provide and facilitate the proper learning environment and stimuli that cultivate and nourish the mind.

There are innumerable types of brainteasers and puzzles. Many can be found in books, periodicals, or through educational product distributors. In addition, there are marvelous puzzles and brain teasers at our science and technology museums. I would like to offer some that I have found very useful in my math classes.

Logic Problems—Example: James, Sharon and Amin cheer for their home basketball team. Sharon's team's stadium is near two major embassies. Amin lives closer to Sharon than James. The teams are the Washington Bullets, the New Jersey Nets, and the Los Angeles Lakers. Which team does each person cheer for?

Mazes.

Working-Backward Problems—The Blue Bears have the ball on their own 2-yard line. They made a nice gain on their first play. Then they lost 7 yards on the next play. The tailback ran for a 12-yard gain, but they were penalized and lost 14 yards. The next play was a 25-yard pass that was completed at the 48-yard line. How many yards did the Blue Bears make on their first play?

Optical Illusions.

Problem-Solving Puzzles—Example: A group of hikers must cross a river. The bridge is out, and the river is wide. Suddenly, the group notices two boys playing in a tiny rowboat. The boat will only hold two boys or one hiker—not a boy and a hiker. All the same, the group succeeds in crossing the river in the boat. How?

CHAPTER THREE: RELEVANCY THROUGH APPLICATIONS

The main reason for the minimal interest that Black students display and possess toward learning mathematics is that they do not see the relevance nor the importance that math has to their reality and world. Many students lack the desire and drive to be proficient in mathematics because they see it as something you have to learn in order to progress to the next educational level. Many students come to math class every day with questions on their minds such as: "Why am I learning this?" "How is this going to help me in my life?" "Who cares about all of this?" Due to the current focus and aim of today's mathematics education, these questions raised by students go unanswered. In most mathematics classrooms the focus and rationale for learning mathematics is twisted and off-base. Mathematics instructors give students thousands of algorithms, procedures, and rules that are not supported by any real meaning or relevance. Therefore, mathematics becomes, in the mind of the student, a complicated concoction of symbols, operations, numbers, and variables that are abstract and perplexing.

This problem stems form a misunderstanding of the aim and basis of mathematical study. Mathematics is a science that has at its core the potential solution to many real-world problems. The entire scope and purpose for learning mathematics is to equip the student with the proper tools and materials needed to solve problems he or she encounters. Hence, mathematical modeling and the use of applications must become the major scope, aim, and mission of all mathematics teachers. Otherwise, we are doing a major disservice to the student, as well as to mathematics education.

The teacher must show students the universality of mathematics. There is hardly any discipline, field, or profession that does not use the application and practicality of mathematics. Students must be taught that mathematics exists in nature, sports, music, art, architecture, science, economics, business, and the list goes on. Once students can connect their individual aspirations to be doctors, lawyers, artists, or businesspeople to the science of mathematics, they will gain greater interest in math and desire to master it, which will ultimately lead to higher performance academically.

Since Black children are already preoccupied with so many other things, it is extremely difficult to attract and capture their attention. This is where teaching the universality of mathematics becomes useful. Black children love sports, music, art, video games, and other forms of entertainment. In each of these activities, mathematics is significant and relevant. Teachers can harness the love and attraction that students have for sports and entertainment and transform it into a love and attraction for mathematics. All the teacher need do is integrate the sports and entertainment worlds into the mathematics curriculum and lesson plan. When students can visualize the pertinence and significance that mathematics has to the things they love to do, they will begin to be more attracted and inspired to learn and study mathematics.

There are many ways and methods by which this can be accomplished. One method is to provide more focus and attention to problem solving than we normally do. In most math classes across the country, problem solving and mathematical modeling is given minimum concentration and focus. Problem solving is taught as if it were a separate branch of mathematics or as if it were optional to the mathematics curriculum. In order to properly teach mathematics and stimulate our students to excel and progress in the real world, we educators must reposition problem-solving and mathematical modeling from the back seat to the forefront. We must revolutionize mathematics education in such a way that solving real-world problems and applications becomes the fruit of the mathematics tree and not just a leaf. Not only are most math curricula deficient in problem solving but also most math textbooks do not focus on real-world problems or mathematical modeling unless you order a textbook that specializes in these areas. When students do see word problems or applications in the textbook, they are relegated to a small section of the text or are so minimal they become meaningless. Therefore, teachers will have to procure supplemental material on problem solving and mathematical modeling in order to be effective. There are books and periodicals that focus solely on these subjects. A problem that I noticed with the major textbooks and supplementary material on problem solving is that most if not all of the word problems deal with the reality and lives of middle-class White people. Black students will find it hard to be motivated and inspired by problems involving people and situations that are foreign and alien to their reality. So, one very important aspect of teaching problem solving and mathematical modeling is to make sure the problems and situations are relevant to Black students. This can be accomplished by simply changing the word problems around or altering the names, places, or activities to fit the world of the Black student.

Since many Black students live in a reality that may not be of positive nature due to poverty, crime, and negative stereotypes, it is important for the mathematics teacher to use mathematics itself as a means of raising the self-esteem, confidence, and aspirations of students. One way this can be accomplished is to construct word problems or mathematical models that instill positive goals and aspirations as well as motivate and inspire students to make changes in society.

For example, I develop my own word problems and models because of the lack of inclusion of Black reality in most mathematics textbooks. I also try to motivate my students to choose careers and goals that will elevate the condition of Black people. Here are a few sample word problems that I have used with my students. It is crucial for teachers to develop the creativity to design mathematical activities and materials of their own.

Sample 1

Jamil is the owner of Proud to Be Black Men's Store. He notices a customer who buys a pair of shoes, which are regularly priced at $360.00 but are on sale for 25% off. The customer also buys a $780.00 leather coat, which is on sale for 15 % off. What will be the total cost to the customer?

Sample 2

Rhonda is a farmer who has just purchased a new seeding machine that can seed 33 acres in 14 hours. Her farm contains a total of 100 acres. How long will it take Rhonda to seed the entire farm using the new machinery?

Sample 3

David is an electrical engineer who has been called to the Asiatic Shoe Factory to solve a problem. At the factory, the main generator produces 200 2/3 megawatts of electricity. There are five machines that receive an equal amount of electricity from the generator. David tells the owner that in order for a machine to operate safely, at least 45 megawatts of electricity are required. Will David find that the 5 machines operate safely? Why or why not?

Sample 4

You are a brain surgeon at Elijah Muhammad Hospital. A patient comes in with a brain tumor measuring 3 cm in width. You have to prescribe medicine for him and you need to determine the correct dosage. Using the formula $D = 7.5w-8$, how many milliliters of medicine should you give the patient? (D=dosage amount, W=width of brain tumor)

As you can see in the few sample problems I have provided, the word problems illustrate to Black students that the careers and professions they might seek, require the use of mathematics and science. They also involve Black people who are the owners and operators of their own businesses and companies, thereby instilling a desire for students to become self-sufficient.

Black children are bombarded with images and role models that are either negative or involve sports, play, and entertainment. This creates in Black children a belief that the only things they can become proficient in and master must be in the areas of sports and entertainment. Most schools do not motivate or steer Black children toward careers and pursuits that require high academic and scholastic performance and aptitude. Thus, Black students are not motivated to excel in the sciences, mathematics, literary fields, and professions. The media compounds the problem by neglecting to portray Blacks in these fields, while at the same time they portray an enormous number of Blacks in negative and demeaning roles. If students do not see members of their community in the fields of science and mathematics, they conclude that they do not possess the ability or the intellect to master these fields. Hence, most Black students lack the confidence, faith, and self-esteem that is required to overcome the difficulty factor involved in the study of science or mathematics.

I attempt, through the construction and development of different types of word problems and mathematical modeling, exercises, and activities, to destroy this false belief in our children and encourage them to pursue the most difficult careers and professions. We as mathematics teachers possess an abundance of power and influence. We can reshape and remold Black students minds, break down the barriers that society has erected, and free our students to become whatever their abilities can encompass.

In addition to providing students with word problems and mentioning applications of math in the real world, teachers may also develop learning activities and projects that teach the relevancy of mathematics to the real world. These types of activities will help in the retention of material because they require students to be creative as well as develop and construct learning materials on their own. When students create, design, and develop projects of their own, they are more apt to remember and retain the mathematics that are involved in the projects and activities.

Activity 1—Business Day

When teaching percents and decimals, have the students formulate their own business, with a list of prices for each of their items. The students should design their stores on poster boards or use a cardboard box as a display. There should also be certain items that are on sale at each of the students stores at discount percentages. Each student should bring their store display to class, where other students will play the roles of cashier and customer. The task of the cashier is to determine the amount the customer owes, take the paper and coin play money, and return any change that is due the customer. This activity teaches children how to add and subtract decimals and also how to deal with percentages to find the discount prices. Students also learn the science of business management and administration, along with this application of math.

Activity 2—Integer Boxing

When teaching algebra, students must learn how to compare integers. One fun and exciting technique begins with bringing two students to the front of the class. Each student picks a card from a special deck. Each card has an integer and a sign (negative or positive) on it. After the students pick their cards, they face the class and display them. The teacher then plays the role of a prizefight announcer and pretends that the two students are about to have a boxing match. The students do not actually box, but the rest of the class must use the rules for comparing integers to decide which student won the fight. For example, if one student picked a positive 3 and another chose negative three, who won? Or one student selected negative 99 and another chose negative one, who won? This simple but fun activity will teach students how to compare integers, and it will also enhance their retention of the skill because they are learning from interaction in an exciting activity. The abnormal mode in which they were taught helps their retention enormously. The more something is out of the ordinary, the easier it is to remember. When the students encounter comparing integers in the future, they will remember the pretend boxing activity and how much fun it was.

Activity 3—Metric Pizza

Students have a hard time learning the metric system because they have to memorize a lot of conversion tables. If the metric system could come alive to them, it would be easier to learn and more enjoyable to use. One way this can be achieved is to have students bring in the ingredients needed to make a homemade pizza. The teacher should have the students break into groups and begin following a metric recipe for pizza, which the teacher supplies. As the students follow the directions, they will be required to translate the metric quantities into our North American weights and measures in order to use the measuring scales, cups, and spoons they brought from home. This will help them understand metric dimensions while, at the same time, they apply mathematics to the real world.

Project 1— Scale Drawings

One excellent way to teach students scale factors and scale drawings is to have students design the blueprint for something they would like to build. The students will play the role of architects and make a scale drawing. The students will first calculate drawing measurements, using the scale they developed. For example, if a student designs a skyscraper, he could calculate the actual height it would be in the real world using the scale he developed. This project not only teaches students how to use proportions and scale factors but also teaches them some plane geometry and encourages them to be creative and industrious. Students retention will be enhanced since they are developing and constructing something of their own. They will always remember what they developed and its correlation to mathematics.

Project 2—Circle Graphs

I have found that students love to develop their own circle graphs. For this project, have the students set-up a business or corporation of their own. Students should then develop an annual budget amount that they will need to operate their business or corporation. The teacher should be sure to explain this aspect to the students by presenting them with examples. The students will then identify departments in their corporation or business that require funds in order to operate. The students will also design circle graphs, using poster board and making them visually and graphically pleasing to the eye. After students design and draw the circle graphs, they will use mathematics to determine the correct percentages of the budget that each area or department will receive. For example, if a student is going to be in the restaurant business, she will need to determine—and visualize on the graph—the percentage of budget money apportioned to areas such as advertising, payroll, food and supplies, cleaning and sanitation, and research and development. This is a wonderful and exciting project that forces the student to make critical decisions and choices and provides them with an opportunity to apply math to the real world.

Project 3—Circular Architecture

Geometry is a branch of mathematics that requires the ability to think critically and visualize properly. I have always tried to give the students something interesting and exciting to illuminate the geometry curriculum, which, to most students, seems boring and vague. When teaching a unit on circles, I ask the students to design a building using only circles. They can choose from a school, hospital, corporate building, or library. The students play the role of architects and design blueprints for their buildings. This project stimulates the students spatial and visualization skills as well as enhances their problem-solving abilities. Since most buildings contain straight lines and planes, the students have to delve deep into their creative minds to come up with an appropriate design. The difficulty and creativeness of this project stimulates the desire and motivation in students that we educators have been searching for.

The mathematics teacher is not limited to using word problems or creating activities and projects in order to show students the relevancy of mathematics. You can also utilize field trips and guest speakers. Black students usually do not experience educational field trips or leaving the confines of their neighborhoods or communities. Yet, field trips can be a valuable help in teaching mathematics.

Field trips can involve traveling to museums, businesses, or other places where mathematics is utilized. Science museums, aeronautical or aerospace museums, factories, nuclear or electrical plants, engineering and architectural firms, biological and chemical laboratories, hospitals, sporting events, art museums, and musical performances are just a few of the places where you can take children to illustrate to them how mathematics is used in our world. A field trip to a park or forest is an excellent way to show the connection between mathematics and nature. Students can learn about the mathematics involved in determining the age of trees, the symmetry of plant life and rocks, or the mathematical formula used to calculate the number of chirps a cricket will make in a given amount of time, depending upon the weather.

An important field trip destination is a weather station to see how meteorologists utilize mathematics to predict the weather, study earthquakes and volcanoes, and monitor hurricanes and tornadoes. There are so many places we can take the children because mathematics is everywhere. Field trips are wonderful ways to give students a greater appreciation for mathematics and the universe.

In addition to taking students out of the classroom, another excellent method is to invite guest speakers from different fields and disciplines into the classroom. This will allow people from outside the classroom to bear witness to the power that mathematics has in the world.

These speakers can share what they do in their particular fields and how mathematics plays an integral and crucial part in their work. People such as accountants, sports figures, entertainers, doctors, plumbers, carpenters, electricians, biologists, and chemists are all excellent guests for the mathematics classroom.

Chapter Four:
Animation and Creativity

One major aspect of my teaching style, which I have found to be very successful and effective, is my ability to be animated and creative in my presentation of material. Whenever I teach, I try to be very lively, animated, enthusiastic, and humorous. Every class becomes a "performance" of mathematics.

Black students are accustomed to watching television, listening to music, playing video games, and going to the theater. All of these forms of entertainment provide our students with stimulation and pleasure. Therefore, I try to utilize the same format when I teach. I want the students to watch me explain mathematics as though they were watching television or their favorite movie. I try to capture from them the same degree of devotion and attention that they give to sports and entertainment programs. It is all accomplished through the animation and creativity that I integrate into my lesson plans and activities.

There is an old saying in selling, that to be a good salesman you must first sell yourself, and you must believe in the product you are selling. I attempt to follow this principle each time I address my students. The students must see that I believe in myself and that I love the subject that I am trying to teach them. We as teachers cannot expect students to be motivated, inspired, and encouraged to learn if we are not fanatical and excited about it ourselves. We must come alive and express the excitement that we feel about mathematics and teaching. When we do this, we pass desire to learn and motivation on to our students and receive back from them immediate transformations, manifested by increased attention span, interest, enthusiasm, and the will to learn.

I come to class every day as though I were on my own television program trying to stimulate and inspire the audience to master mathematics. I attempt to create an environment and an atmosphere that stimulates students' interest through my body language, gestures, personality, and humor. I transmit love, kindness, and empathy to my students, which elicits from them a positive manner toward the lesson and me. My entire focus is to present mathematics to the students in an exciting format that creates in them a desire and drive to attend my class just as if it were their favorite movie or television program.

Math teachers must recognize the fact that most Black students have a preconceived dislike for mathematics and are anything but excited or stimulated when they hear that it is time to learn math. This is why it is incumbent upon the teacher to bring motivation, animation, and stimulation into the classroom if we are to change students' perceptions and attitudes about mathematics. We must be creative in our lesson planning, presentation, and development of learning activities. You cannot be a textbook robot or a worksheet copier and expect students to be stimulated and motivated in your classroom.

One way I bring life and enlightenment into my class is through the creation and use of mathematical games and activities. These games and creative activities teach mathematics through competition, fun, and excitement. The students already love to play games and to compete. When you use games and other fun activities in the classroom, you will not have a problem stimulating and inspiring students to participate in the learning process. The only problem you might have is explaining to them that the game must end because time is up.

There are many mathematical games that you can find in books or periodicals, but I have found that the best ones come from the creative mind of the teacher. The games I use are effective because I incorporate what the students love to do outside of school into the activity or game, which, of course, contains the mathematical concept or skill.

Over the years, I have created and developed various mathematical games that have done wonders in terms of stimulating, inspiring, and motivating students. When they are involved in the game or competitive activity, they exert 100 percent effort and dedication to the mathematics involved while, at the same time, they enjoy themselves tremendously. Here are a few examples of games that I have developed through the years. You may apply them in your classroom where and when you see fit or alter them to facilitate your needs.

MATH ALIEN INVADERS

Alien Invaders is a game that can be utilized for a classroom or homework assignment. It is similar to a popular video game entitled Space Invaders. This game can be used to teach most mathematical concepts and skills. The teacher must first draw the game board and decide how many problems he/she would like the student to solve. After the quantity of problems is determined, the teacher draws a like number of alien creatures. The aliens should be scattered across the top and in the middle of the board, as if they were descending from the sky. The idea is that the students are fighters for their own planet, and these invaders must not land or the planet will be destroyed.

Under each alien, there is written a math problem, exemplifying the skill or concept the teacher would like to teach. It could be an arithmetic problem, an algebraic equation, or a simplification problem. The teacher can be as creative as he wants when drawing and designing the game board.

At the bottom of the game board there is a list of answers to every problem on the board, and above each answer there is a letter of the alphabet representing the answer. Photocopies of the game board are passed out to the students. The students must decide which is the correct answer to each problem and place the letter representing it next to the alien in order to destroy it.

Have students use colored markers to mark the letters they choose. The teacher collects the paper and checks whether the correct letter has been placed next to each alien. If the student answers four or more problems incorrectly, it means that the aliens have landed and the planet has been destroyed.

WHEEL OF MATH

This is an offshoot of the popular Wheel of Fortune game show. The teacher should break the students up into teams of three or four. A scorekeeper can be selected or the teacher can keep score. The students really get involved when the teacher plays the role of game show host.

The game begins with the teacher choosing a word puzzle and placing the blank spaces, which represent the letters that will solve the puzzle, on the board. Then the teacher provides the class with a clue to solving the puzzle, which may be a phrase, person, place, event, or thing.

The teacher then gives each team a math problem to solve. The first team to solve their problem goes first. All of the teams must solve their problems. The team that is in action chooses a letter, which they think might help solve the word puzzle, or they can attempt to solve the entire puzzle all at once. If they present an incorrect answer, then the next team may render their answer.

When the letter chosen is among the letters in the puzzle, that team receives a point for each time that letter comes up. If a team is able to solve the entire puzzle, they receive four points. The game continues in this manner until the puzzle is solved, or until a predetermined time limit is reached, and the team with the highest score wins. The teacher should be sure to use puzzle topics that are familiar to the students.

MATH BASKETBALL

In this game, students will pair up and compete against each other. The teacher should have the students arrange their desks in such a manner that each student faces his or her opponent. Each pair of students is given a sheet of paper containing a miniature basketball court. The court should be nearly the size of the paper. The game sheet will consist of a drawing of a basketball court. Each student will also receive a set of mathematical questions and problems. For example, you may give them problems that require them to find percents, solve equations, multiply or divide decimals, or find derivatives. Along with the set of problems, each student will also receive an answer sheet.

The teacher should also give each student an object such as a coin or a block to represent his or her position on the game sheet. Each pair of participants will also receive a cube with a + or a - on each face. These symbols represent a made shot or a missed shot. The symbols should be distributed equally so that you have three of each on the cube.

The game begins with the students flipping a coin to determine who will have the ball first. The student who wins the coin toss goes first. The student then selects the correct answer to one of the math problems given to him by the other student from his problem sheet. If the answer given is correct, the student will role the cube to determine if his shot is successful or missed. If the student misses the shot, his opponent gets the ball. The game continues in this format until someone reaches a designated score.

MATH BASEBALL

Math Baseball is similar to Math Basketball. However, instead of playing on a game sheet illustrating a basketball court, students play on a game sheet illustrating a baseball diamond. Students pair up and sit facing each other just as in Math Basketball. Each student receives 9 blocks or coins to represent his players. A cube with the following letters on it are given to each pair of students: 1 D for a double, 1 S for a single, 1 T for a triple, 1 H for a home run, and 2 Os for "outs." Just as in Math Basketball, the students receive a problem sheet and an answer sheet.

The game begins by flipping a coin to determine who will bat first. The student who loses the coin toss gives a problem to the other student. If the student answers the problem correctly, he rolls the cube. If he rolls an S, he places one of his coins or blocks on first base; if he rolls a D, he places a coin or block on second base, and so on. However, if he rolls an O, he receives an out and is required to solve another problem. The game continues until the player receives three outs; then the game switches and the other student is given problems to solve. The game is finished when time is up or when a player reaches a designated score.

SIMULATIONS AND ROLE PLAYING

Another creative method that can illuminate a mathematics classroom is to integrate simulations and role-playing into the lessons and activities. Role-playing is an excellent way to bring the real world into the math classroom.

Students can play the roles of doctors, lawyers, engineers, architects, businesspeople, scientists, meteorologists, newscasters, and farmers. The students will gain an understanding of how each of these professionals applies mathematics in his or her field. When they can see the many fields and professions that utilize math on an everyday basis, students will be inspired to want to learn mathematics.

In addition to teaching students relevancy, role-playing provides stimulation, enthusiasm, and motivation. Students enjoy role-playing because they are simulating adults. They have the desire at an early age to act out adult roles and tasks. By adding role-playing activities to the math class, the teacher is able to harness the energy and excitement the students possess about playing adult roles, and transmit that same energy into proficiency and mastery of mathematics. We all know that children love to play doctor, fireman, lawyer, or chef for a day. Now, they will be able to transfer that same love and desire into learning mathematical concepts, skills, and principles.

There are many careers, professions, and aspects of life that can be used in role-playing and simulations in the math classroom. I would like to offer a few examples that you might use.

GEOMETRY COURT

One of the most difficult and abstract aspects of geometry are the two-column proofs. Because many students find them difficult to do, boring, and irrelevant, I try to spice up my lessons on two-column proofs by encouraging them to simulate a courtroom session. Each student is assigned a role to play. One student plays the role of judge. Several students are assigned the roles of lawyers, and the rest are assigned to play the role of jury.

The lawyers are assigned different geometric proofs that they will have to write in two-column form. On the day of the activity, the lawyers present their proofs to the judge and jury as if they were presenting their arguments in an actual courtroom. After each lawyer is finished, the jury decides whether the two-column proof was valid and correct. They render a verdict of guilty if the proof was incorrectly done, or they render a verdict of innocent if the proof was correctly done. The student representing the judge makes the final decision and pronounces the sentence for each guilty student.

The teacher should be sure to pick the best student to represent the judge. The more teacher creativity, the more fun and excitement the students will have. This activity will lead to a greater understanding of two-column proofs and a longer retention of the material.

ENGINEER

There are many projects that ask students to play the role of engineers. One project that is excellent for the geometry class requires students to design and construct bridges to see whose bridge can hold the most weight. This project demonstrates to students which geometric shapes and figures are most appropriate for withstanding pressure and stress. It also enhances and cultivates the creativity and problem-solving potential that lies within each student.

Another excellent project is to have students locate something in the world that can be improved, and then develop and construct ways for doing this. The students should write reports and provide research and a visual presentation to illustrate and demonstrate how they can improve the existing problem. Some examples that can be used include: traffic jams, long waiting lines, deaths due to high-rise fires, destruction caused by earthquakes, and deaths by car accidents. This project requires students to apply mathematics to the real world and exposes them to the types of problems an engineer or scientist may encounter.

TALK SHOW

When reviewing concepts, skills, vocabulary, or properties in a unit or chapter, one superb method that can be used to grasp students' attention and motivate them at the same time is to simulate a talk show. I use this activity when I am introducing a new chapter or unit or when I am reviewing at the end of a chapter or unit. This format stimulates students to relearn what they were taught, and it helps them retain information. The students love to play the roles of participants on a talk show or the talk show host. This activity creates an enormous desire and drive in the students to learn and participate since the activity involves something they enjoy and love.

Here's how it works: The teacher plays the role of the talk show host. Students are chosen to play the roles of guests on the show. The classroom should be arranged to resemble a television talk show set. Each student serving as a guest is given a mathematical concept, rule, or property to present and answer questions on. Students may also be given certain sections or parts of a chapter or unit to present. The students should be allowed a day or two to study the parts they are given so they can adequately present the material and will be equipped to answer the questions. The rest of the students who are not chosen as special guests play the talk show audience. The audience will prepare questions and make comments on the presentation.

The show begins with the teacher introducing herself and the topic or chapter that will be discussed. Then the teacher introduces each student and the area of expertise he or she represents. The student then presents his subject and opens the floor for questions. In this simulation, students not only play the role of talk show participants but they also experience switching teacher-student roles. By allowing the students to play the role of teacher, you will provide them with a greater appreciation of the teacher's job and a deeper understanding of the difficulty involved in trying to explain material and information.

MEDICAL SIMULATION

The last role-playing activity that I would like to offer involves students playing the role of physicians. Teachers will find this activity appropriate and practical for a unit on functions and graphing. Students play the role of physicians and take turns measuring the height and weight of the other students in the class. The students gather all the data and organize it into a table or chart.

The teacher instructs the students that weight will be the independent variable and height the dependent variable. Students are asked to plot the data on a coordinate graph, graphing weight on the x-axis and height on the y-axis. Then students analyze the information on the graph to see if they notice a relationship. When they realize that there is a relationship, they try to describe it by writing the equation of the line. The teacher may aid the students in finding the slope and y-intercept of the data on the graph to enable them to produce the equation of the line.

Students will discuss why they feel there is a relationship and why the graph either verifies or invalidates their conclusions. Students will also write a report on how physicians can utilize the equation of the line to help them make critical decisions and write prescriptions for future patients.

I love this role-playing exercise because it not only gives students a clearer and deeper understanding of the concepts of a function but also illustrates to the students how mathematics is applied in the medical field.

CHAPTER FIVE:
COMMUNICATION AND
EVALUATION

Educating Black children is a task and mission that requires great sensitivity, caution, and delicacy. Most Black children come to school with numerous domestic and personal problems. Many are from single-parent settings and abusive homes, homes where domestic violence or drug use is prevalent. Many of our children come from poverty-stricken homes. We cannot dismiss the fact that a child will likely experience difficulty in learning if he or she comes from these types of backgrounds and environments.

In addition to the prevalence of negative home environments, Black children must also battle the everyday bombardment of negative stereotypes and vicious attacks on their self-worth, self-esteem, and self-confidence. All of these factors and more are reasons why teachers must be careful and cautious in how they communicate with Black students. It is critical for us as teachers to analyze and monitor our manner and conduct with the students because the attitude of the student has a direct effect on their motivation and desire to learn.

We educators can either communicate with the student in a positive way, providing healing to the wounds that society and the home have inflicted, or we can further damage the student with harmful communication.

HOW TO TEACH MATH TO BLACK STUDENTS

Unfortunately, by mishandling and mistreating the students because of ignorance or lack of concern, many teachers are exacerbating the existing problems that the student brings to school. This is one reason why you rarely hear a student name his teachers as heroes or role models. However, there is hope that this reality can be reversed.

One aspect of communication that we, as educators, must become aware of is the area of nonverbal communication. Students are very perceptive of an instructor who cares nothing about their welfare, education, or well-being. Vibrations of negativity and insensitivity can be easily detected and identified by the teacher's body language, gestures, and overall posture and personality. This is why it is incumbent upon the teacher to display the type of nonverbal communication that radiates concern, empathy, and kindness.

In order to teach Black students who are already wounded by society and a destructive home environment, teachers must take a genuine interest in each student's academic performance, social and intellectual development, and moral and spiritual well-being. We cannot take the position that we are only teachers and whatever happens to the child outside of the classroom is irrelevant and insignificant to us. Each student must become an integral part of our lives to the extent that we go beyond the call of duty to aid, support, and develop our students so they can reach their full potential.

Communication and Evaluation

Once the teacher begins to internalize these principles of concern, care, and help, students will begin to see the illuminations of the teacher's spirit and feel the transmission of love, sympathy, and kindness. The teacher's nonverbal communication will especially benefit students who are suffering from low self-esteem, low self-confidence, and depression. Teachers do not realize the awesome power and force we can exercise to transform a student from a destructive, depressive mentality to one of hope, confidence, and faith.

Here are some ways that we can transmit positive nonverbal communication.

1. Maintain a beautiful spirit about yourself.

2. Never transmit negative body language or use disrespectful gestures or looks.

3. Never show feelings of disgust, disappointment, or intolerance toward students through facial expressions, body language, or gestures.

4. Use body language, gestures, and facial expressions that demonstrate feelings of love, generosity, care, and concern.

HOW TO TEACH MATH TO BLACK STUDENTS

Verbal communication is crucial to properly instructing Black students as well. Students weigh every word that comes out of the teacher's mouth. Since the teacher is viewed as an authority figure, every word that we speak is considered valid and reliable. Therefore, teachers cannot spew words of negativity to a child and expect them not to cause severe damage to the child's psyche later. The teacher's perspective of a child will color the child's perspective of him or herself. That is why it is critical for the teacher to closely monitor the verbal communication directed to the students.

Teachers must cease using negative and degrading comments toward students who are already psychologically damaged by society and destructive home environments. Many Black children suffer from verbal and sometimes physical abuse. They perceive themselves from a negative viewpoint and lack the proper motivation, inspiration, and confidence needed to perform well academically. This is where mathematics teachers can intervene and administer assistance and aid to help these problems.

Teachers must first work to extinguish all negative verbal communication and interactions with the students. Even when a student disappoints a teacher or is not maintaining proper department standards, negativity and verbal abuse must not enter into the teacher-student relationship as a means of punishment. On the contrary, the math class must be full of positivity, love, joy, and inspiration. Regardless of the student's academic and behavioral background, the teacher must provide positive reinforcement and stimulation to the extent that confidence is built and the child begins to feel good about himself. We know as educators about the self-fulfilling prophecy of failure. In order to turn this prophecy around in the math class, we must bombard each student with positive communication and esteem-building interaction.

The Black student faces a world that is against his advancement and well-being. There are numerous media sources as well as societal and home factors that tear down the spirit, esteem, and confidence of the Black child. Many Black children digest daily messages of inferiority, negativity, and attacks on their self-esteem and self-worth. This produces an inferiority complex that ultimately leads to a lack of will, desire, and confidence in terms of excelling and mastering mathematics. We teachers must do whatever is in our power to combat and destroy these negative mind-sets of Black students and utilize positive communication to instill into them confidence, faith, and a strong will to succeed.

Mathematics teachers have a tremendous challenge and obstacle to overcome because Black children not only possess an overall negative perception of self but most believe that being Black is directly related to mathematical illiteracy.

Black students do not perceive themselves as performing well or possessing the mental capacity to master mathematics because they do not see images of Blacks in their math textbooks, nor do they see any Black mathematicians in their communities or on television.

In order for Black students to have faith and confidence in their mathematical ability, they must see examples and role models who have mastered and contributed to mathematics. Black students today are steered and motivated by society, parents, and the educational system to seek excellence in sports and entertainment. This causes a serious void in the number of Black students inspired to pursue careers and professions involving competency and literacy in mathematics and science.

It is imperative that the teacher's verbal communication has a positive and uplifting nature. The mathematics teacher must transform Black students' minds that are frozen in false thoughts of doubt and uncertainty. The only way this can be accomplished is through feeding the dormant power that lies within every student. Positive verbal communication cultivates and nourishes each student's will while, at the same time, it destroys and extinguishes doubt, fear, and uncertainty.

Here are some examples of positive verbal communication that can be used in the classroom.

Communication and Evaluation

1. Always give students tasks and assignments in a manner that transmits confidence in their ability. Use phrases such as: "I know you can do this," "I expect nothing but the best from you," and "I am sure you will do a wonderful job on this."

2. Use positive words to correct students when they make mistakes or fall short of your expectations. Examples: "That's not quite right, but you are very close," "That was a good response, but not quite what I was looking for," "Thank you for your effort, but you might be looking at it incorrectly."

3. Stay away from negative words in response to an incorrect answer or remark. For example, do not use phrases such as: "That is absolutely wrong," "How could you say something like that?" "You're just not cut-out for this class," "It's no wonder you are failing with answers like this."

4. Compliment the student whenever possible. For example: "That was an excellent response," "You will make a wonderful doctor, businessman, engineer, or scientist," "You did a beautiful job on this assignment," and "I am very pleased with your performance."

5. Make references to positive Black role models that have excelled in the fields of mathematics and science.

6. Humor is an excellent means of providing a positive atmosphere and capturing the student's attention.

A subtle form of communication and interaction between teacher and student that must be analyzed and discussed is the evaluation of students' performance. Communication, whether positive or negative, occurs each time the teacher makes a written or verbal assessment of students. Since we have already touched on verbal assessments, we want to look at how we can improve on written assessments and evaluations.

Often, mathematics teachers simply mark a student's paper with red ink and "Xs." Teachers also mark a letter or number grade on papers. For students who are struggling in mathematics, this type of evaluation and assessment can be degrading, depressive, and destructive. We have already discussed the delicate and fragile ego of most Black students, so we can easily see how marking a student's paper with a big "D" or "F" can do serious harm. If the student sees only negative marks and grades on a continuous basis, the student begins to doubt himself, and his desire to improve is undermined. Marking a student's paper with letters and symbols that imply value judgments does not allow them to understand the reason why the answers were incorrect nor does it provide them with the skills to achieve correct answers.

There are many other forms of evaluation and assessment that do not produce feelings of low self-worth and low self-confidence in students. One method is to assign a letter grade or a number grade, but not allow students to see the grade on their papers. Instead, the teacher can use phrases to describe to the student how well or how badly she did. Use words such as: satisfactory work, good try, needs a little improvement, keep on trying. The teacher should use phrases that do not represent total failure or inability on the student's part. Words such as: poor, fail, wrong, or below average should not be used. These words and others like them do not take into consideration the student's effort or potential to learn. Students may not get enough answers correct or understand a certain rule or skill, but if they give maximum effort or make their best attempt, they should be praised and recognized.

Too often, the student perceives low grades as a sign of inability or incompetence. Teachers can either reinforce this fallacy or change the thinking to the student's betterment. Teachers should evaluate and assess students so that the students perceive a low grade as evidence of lack of maximum preparation and study as opposed to a flaw or defect in their intellect or mental capacity. Preparation and study time are elements of good academic performance: something students have total control over and can improve. If students can correlate their below-average performance with improper preparation and an insufficient amount of effort, they will see that they can improve on their grades while maintaining their self-confidence and motivation to learn. Therefore, teachers should remind students when they perform below standards, that they simply need to prepare better at home and dedicate more time and effort toward the material. This is a better approach to evaluation and assessment than to label the student as learning disabled, a slow-learner, or unintelligent.

Another method of grading students that can assist in improving a student's esteem and self-confidence is to provide partial credit to students who may not give a correct answer because they made simple and careless mistakes in calculation or simplification. Many students comprehend the mathematical concepts and rules, but they make careless mistakes in working out the problems. Teachers should provide partial credit whenever possible to those students who display comprehension of mathematics but make mistakes in their work.

COMMUNICATION AND EVALUATION

The teacher must also be cognizant of those students who may understand the material but have difficulty articulating and expressing it on a written test. Many Black students have difficulty taking certain types of tests because Black children learn differently, in certain areas, than other students. Because of this fact, teachers need to design and develop alternative evaluation methods to allow those students who may not do well on written tests a chance to demonstrate their proficiency in another mode or format.

Oral presentations, visual presentations, reports, research papers, projects, and classroom participation are just a few ways in which students can be evaluated. We discussed in an earlier chapter how the most important aspect of mathematics is its application to the real world. This can serve as another means of evaluating students. If the student cannot follow a certain algorithm, theorem, or rule on a written exam but can explain how the math applies in the real world, that has to be looked at as a demonstration of comprehension and understanding of mathematics.

In summary, the mathematics teacher must be sensitive to and cognizant of the various environmental factors that affect the way Black children learn. We must structure our teaching methodology and learning environment in a way that complements the social, psychological, and spiritual makeup of the student. Communication, whether it is verbal, nonverbal, or in the form of evaluation and assessment, is an extremely important and crucial component in the success or failure of a student's education.

CHAPTER SIX:
THE POWER OF THE SENSES

No one can deny the tremendous effect that our environment has on molding and shaping the minds of our children. Our children's minds are filled with a variety of television programming, music and entertainment videos, and music lyrics. Almost every Black student is familiar with the latest music video, video game, popular television show, or recent motion picture.

The architects and engineers of these various forms of entertainment have mastered the appeal to the senses and virtually control the attention of the majority of Black youth. If we, as math instructors, could harness just a fraction of the attention and motivation that youth give to these various forms of entertainment, we could produce mathematical geniuses overnight. It is wise for us to study and analyze the reasons why our children are so attracted to these forms of entertainment and see how we can incorporate the same techniques into our classrooms. Let's look at the different senses that are stimulated by the entertainment industry, which engulfs our children's minds on a daily basis.

The premiere sense is the sense of sight. The television, motion pictures, and videos that Black children watch influence them through their visual sense. The mere fact that a student can provide a word-for-word and scene-by-scene analysis of a movie, television program, or video demonstrates the power of the visual sense in terms of learning, memory, and retention. The entertainment media provide stimulation and learning that we as educators can only dream of. Imagine if mathematics education could be the basis of a television show, a movie, or a video. Imagine if mathematics could receive the same amount of attention, motivation, inspiration, and dedication that today's youth give to the entertainment industry. Well, we don't have to imagine and dream anymore. There are ways to duplicate this phenomenon in the math class. The following is a list of a few of the ways that math instructors can utilize visual power to teach math.

1. Use number lines, thermometers, navigation charts, and sample pictures of savings and checking account receipts when teaching integers.

2. Use paintings, architectural blueprints, and designs and pictures from nature when teaching geometrical concepts.

3. Drawings, tables, and charts should be used when teaching the metric system. Students will grasp the meaning of units of length, capacity, and weight better when they can visualize these units and make comparisons.

4. Have students design posters, paintings, and advertisements illustrating and promoting some mathematical concept, principle, theorem, or rule.

Another very important sense that is vital to learning
is hearing. Black youth can learn the lyrics of songs in a
matter of minutes. One very popular type of music, rap, allows
children to recite entire songs and retain all the information
in them for extremely long periods of time. This is the ideal
frame of mind we would love to see our students in when it
comes to learning mathematics or any subject. How great
and wonderful would it be to hear students reciting
mathematical formulas, rules, theorems, concepts, and
principles with ease and rapidity? If we could find a way to
encourage our students to memorize, comprehend, and retain
information dealing with mathematics in the same manner
they do their favorite music and song, we could produce
unimaginable excellence and mastery in the field of
mathematics. Well, contrary to what we may think, this can
be accomplished in the mathematics classroom.

Music and song can be excellent tools for teachers to
use to teach mathematics. We are well aware of the attraction
that Black youth have to music. Now the teacher must find
ways to incorporate and integrate the use of music and song
into their lesson plans and activities. In order to do this, the
teacher must study and familiarize himself with the type of

music that the students enjoy. Once an analysis of students' preferences is made, the teacher can use her own creativity to develop songs and musical activities focused around mathematical concepts and rules. For example, you may develop a song on how to subtract fractions using regrouping, or how to change a fraction to a percent, or how to divide or multiply polynomials. The teacher can develop the songs on his own, assigning new words to popular tunes, or he can have students come up with their own songs and lyrics centered on material they learned in class.

As we have said, many Black children are attracted and excited by rap music. The teacher can assign students the job of transforming math concepts, rules, and principles into rap. Then each student can perform his rap in front of the class. As the students rap, they will simultaneously be implanting mathematics into their minds.

Poetry is another form of expression that is attractive to students and can be utilized in teaching mathematics. Students can be encouraged to develop and create poems about the definitions of equivalency, congruency, functions, derivatives, and probability. This activity also stimulates students' critical thinking skills because they must integrate the math into phrases and lines that not only rhyme but also make mathematical sense. Those students who do a good job can have their poems displayed in the class and used to teach future classes the same concepts and definitions.

CHAPTER SEVEN:
BUILDING THE WILL

People everywhere are rapidly coming to recognize the power of their will. Miraculous achievements and exploits have been accomplished solely by the use of one's will power. The technological and scientific advancements made by this generation are evidence that almost anything men and women can conceive in their minds can be brought into existence through the proper utilization of will power.

Imagine what students could achieve in the area of math education if they could tap into the power of their wills. Every child possesses a will that can be directed and used to master mathematics. In order to accomplish this, we must first increase students' desire to learn and engage in mathematics. Lets look at how we can do this.

The will power of a student lies latent and pliant if it is not cultivated, stimulated, and developed. We can think of the process of building the will as similar to the development of muscles. In order to develop muscles, stress and pressure must be applied. The development of will power is similar. Teachers must provide instruction that challenges the students and places pressure on their minds.

Students should be required to practice more and more on solving math problems that inculcate a variety of mathematical concepts and skills, including those that take students to higher and higher difficulty levels. We all know that practice makes perfect. Whatever a student does continually and constantly will become a part of that student's consciousness and will be easier to retain. The math teacher must bombard each student with different types of math content, material, and activities. Just as the weightlifter must increase the amount of work, effort, and pressure on their bodies in order to lift greater weights, the math teacher must increase the students' exposure to different types of problems and challenges in order to set-up their minds as mathematicians. Here are some techniques that teachers can use to increase students exposure to math and challenge their minds.

1. Formulate and develop enrichment exercises and activities that take the students beyond the textbook and stimulate their critical thinking and reasoning skills.

   Examples: a. Students can research and study the use of the metric system in other countries.

   b. Students can study the use of number patterns and sequences in nature and in the world.

   c. Students can study topography as a branch of geometry.

d. Students can study the use of calculus in engineering and science.

e. Students can study the use of math in computer- generated special effects.

2. Have students develop math clubs and organizations where they can discuss math problems, take field trips, and hold debates on math topics and issues, solve math puzzles and paradoxes, and compete in math competitions locally or nationally.

3. Hold math contests and competitions in your school to inspire and motivate students.

4. Provide positive reinforcement and rewards for mastery and high achievement in the math class. Teachers can present plaques, certificates, awards, and other prizes to students who do extremely well. When students see the benefits and consequences of scholastic achievement, they will give greater effort, devotion, and attention to their math work.

5. Teachers should create a student of the week or student of the month award to highlight outstanding and extraordinary math students.

6. Discuss with students their career and occupational goals and aspirations. Discuss the essentiality of mathematics to the fulfillment of their goals.

7. Each math class should provide instruction in consumer math and math for everyday living. This will provide students with a greater appreciation for the rationale and validity of learning mathematics. The more students perceive math as crucial to their everyday survival, the greater the increase in their desire to learn.

8. Teachers should implement the use of computer-assisted instruction into the math class. Black children love to play computer games and are always excited about what they see on the computer or television screen. Therefore, if we use computer games and activities that teach mathematical concepts and skills, students will be overzealous and even vehement about learning math.

Computer games will give students the initiative and skills to solve more and more problems, which, in turn, will build their interest and confidence.

The mathematics curriculum must encompass a wide range of problems and applications centered on each concept. Too often teachers will present mathematical concepts and skills in only one format. Teachers have the responsibility of selecting the type of problems and assignments to give students. We must understand that when students encounter standardized tests, achievement tests, or real-world applications, they will see those same concepts and skills in different formats and problem arrangements. That is why it is incumbent upon the math teacher to teach each math concept and skill, using different types of problems at different levels of difficulty.

For example, when teaching the concept of mean or average, teachers might only present to students the steps and algorithm for calculating the mean of a group of numbers. This is limiting the potential understanding and application of the concept of mean. Teachers need to extend the concept and elevate it to various levels of comprehension and problem solving. An example of a different type of problem arrangement, centered on the same concept, would be to have students solve a problem like this: John scored 75, 80, 90, and 65 on his last four exams. In order to pass biology class, he needs to end up with an average of 80. What must John score on his last exam in order to pass biology? This problem requires students not only to use the methodology for calculating the mean but they must also use algebraic equations and problem-solving skills to come up with the answer. This problem takes the concept of mean to a higher, more complex level and helps to intensify the student's will. The progression in difficulty and complexity also serves to strengthen and build confidence in each student.

No teacher of mathematics should provide students with only one interpretation or use of a math concept or skill. Each concept and skill is pregnant with an enormous array of problems, applications, and interpretations that can be used to evaluate comprehension and proficiency.

Another area that has to be focused on when discussing the topic of building student's will power is the area of confidence. Being confident in one's ability is fundamental to excellence. Any individual who lacks confidence and faith in themselves will find it extremely difficult to channel their will power into accomplishing what they desire.

Black children suffer greatly from this predicament because many lack confidence in themselves, especially as it pertains to dexterity in mathematics and science. There exists an unwritten law in this society that states that Blacks are inferior and less intelligent. This unwritten law has affected the attitudes of Black children to the point where they have fabricated a belief of inferiority that impedes their ability to learn to excel in mathematics.

We educators must turn this around. Math teachers can provide instruction that destroys the inferiority complex that Black students possess and regenerates and revitalizes students' spirit and will to learn. An appropriate classroom environment and methodology can serve to nurture and stimulate students' belief in themselves.

One method that can be utilized to fulfill this task is to provide a detailed review and analysis of solution methods and procedures after each assignment, quiz, or test. Many students lose confidence in themselves when they demonstrate low proficiency and aptitude on a test or quiz. They correlate bad grades with a lack of intelligence on their part or with some flaw or deficiency in their learning ability. When students are able to understand how each problem is solved and the logic behind it, they begin to connect their mistakes to simple misunderstandings or to a lack of concentration rather than to some inadequacy or deficiency.

Teachers can help in this area through the proper construction and implementation of class work and homework assignments. In order to build will power and confidence in the student, teachers should assign problems and activities that allow students to achieve success.

There are always problems that are less difficult than others. Students build confidence in their abilities and proficiency each time they solve problems and answer questions correctly. Each time a student does some problem or assignment in accordance with the teacher's guidelines, his confidence level increases tremendously.

Problem selection and assignment can be balanced out to include simple problems as well as problems that are more difficult. The goal is to randomly give students assignments that ensure that some form of success and achievement occurs.

Furthermore, the more detailed the reviews of problems and test questions the students receive, the less likely it is for students to blame their mistakes on inability or learning deficiency. This in turn will serve to uplift and build confidence back into the students, which will translate into better grades and higher achievement.

The teacher should have each student who fails to meet the standards and criteria laid down in the assignment, quiz, or test analyze and evaluate the rationale behind each error and mistake they made. As students do this, their fear of math will decrease and their understanding of the material will increase. It is also beneficial at times to allow students to redo or retake a quiz or exam that they failed. If they can see an improvement the second time around, they will feel more certain about their ability and potential to succeed. If a math concept is very difficult or complex, balance it with a simple problem or example to allow achievement and a positive outcome to take place.

In conclusion, teachers cannot overlook the extreme importance and relevance of will power and confidence in the mastery of mathematics by Black students. The will of each student must be treated with delicacy, concern, and care in order to provide the proper stimuli and motivation to spark a burning desire in each student to learn and master mathematics.

If we desire to produce mathematical geniuses and scholars, then we must keep in mind a quote by the Honorable Elijah Muhammad, who stated: "Up you mighty nation, you can accomplish what you will." Our students can accomplish what they will as long as we teachers provide the proper encouragement, instruction, and upliftment.

Chapter Eight:
Integrating Subjects Through Simulation and Application

Small World is a wonderfully innovative program, which incorporates and integrates all the major disciplines of an elementary and secondary curriculum into a single unit and project. It is designed to provide students with exposure, comprehension, and mastery of various topics, skills and rules found in mathematics, English, science, and social studies.

The unique part of this program is that teachers can teach and evaluate mastery of skills, objectives, and concepts in a short amount of time and in a more concrete and meaningful manner. Instead of teaching concepts and skills in the various subjects separately from each other, in the Small World program instructors teach integrated skills and concepts on a more comprehensive and practical level.

One major component of this project is its ability to attract and maintain students' interest while at the same time inspiring and motivating them to learn. Students become highly motivated and interested in this program because of its combination of creativity, practicality, and relevance.

The Small World project liberates students from conformity to teaching rules, methods, algorithms, and standards. The students utilize their own free will and creative minds to construct, analyze, design, engineer, and create.

The focus and outcome of this project penetrates to the core of the true purpose and goal of education. Education is designed to extract from the student the creative skills and talents that are embedded deep in his or her consciousness.

SMALL WORLD OBJECTIVES

1. Students will be able to understand, plan, and design their own city.

2. Students will be able to perform basic arithmetic operations, operations with decimals, fractions, and percents, and they will become familiar with basic geometry.

3. Students will be involved in problem solving, reasoning, analyzing, and critical thinking.

4. Students will become familiar with tables, charts, scales, and other measuring devices.

5. Students will be able to convert units in the metric system to our North American system.

6. Students will solve problems involving money, estimation, integers, perimeter, and area.

7. Students will be able to write proposals, laws, rules, policies, and regulations.

8. Students will set up a system for criminal justice, education, sanitation, transportation, commerce, politics, health, and defense.

9. Students will understand and apply concepts of energy, electricity, sewage, agribusiness, conservation, and ecology.

10. Students will be able to understand climate, geography, minerals, and natural resources.

11. Students will appreciate culture, literature, art, and music.

INTRODUCTION

The Small World program is based on a 6-8 week group project involving students planning, designing, and constructing their own city or town. Students take on the roles of various professionals involved in the planning, maintenance, and operations of a city. The program forces students to make major and difficult moral and ethical decisions, which will inculcate principles, concepts, and skills from various areas of study. As students execute each step in the planning, designing, and development of their micro-world, they simultaneously expose their minds to various learning experiences.

IMPLEMENTATION OF PROJECT

The Small World program is designed to be effective with any elementary or secondary class. However, teachers must alter the level of the objectives and activities according to the maturity, reasoning level, and cognitive ability of the students. At the secondary level, this project is more suitable to a 7th or 8th grade curriculum.

Upon introducing the project, the teacher will have the students choose a name and motto for their city. Students will then pick a location on the world map where they would like to build their city. The teacher will question the students on the ramifications of living in the particular area they choose. Questions concerning climate, natural resources, geographic advantages and disadvantages, and political concerns will be discussed with the students.

Integrating Subjects
Through Simulation and Application

After students have agreed on the name, motto, and geographic location, they will discuss plans for developing a blueprint or a written document for implementing each of the following areas. The teacher can take liberties in terms of time spent on each of the following guidelines.

1. A city constitution

2. A code of laws

3. A criminal justice system

4. An educational system—youth and adult

5. A transportation system

6. A sewage and sanitation system

7. Energy and utility programs

8. An economic system

9. A health and hygiene system

10. Conservation of energy program

11. A housing program

12. A department for cultural awareness and Black history

13. Information on food, clothing, and agribusiness

     Students should debate, analyze, and agree on the policies and regulations that will prevail in their city.

     After students have developed a policy for each of the above areas, they next determine an annual budget, which will be the amount needed to properly operate the city. They will then allocate a specific amount for each area of operation. Students then create a circle graph, illustrating the percentage of the budget earmarked for each area.

     The teacher will also question the students on any precautions, special emergency plans, and security measures that they may need to think about and implement.

     The next phase of the project involves the architectural and construction stage. Here, students will decide on a design for their city and will develop a blueprint illustration for roads, bridges, buildings, industries, schools, farms, airports, etc. After the entire city has been planned and the blueprint made, students will break into groups and divide the city into equal parts. Each group will take a part of the city. The groups will calculate measurements, figure out building costs and supplies needed, and make other construction and engineering decisions for their part of the city.

Students are now ready for the last stage of the project, which is the building stage. Using their blueprints, documents, supplies, and materials, they will design and develop a miniature model of their section of the city.

Finally, all of the models are assembled into a complete community.

Because so much learning is going on and so many concepts are being taught, teachers may have different opinions on how to evaluate the students' work. Because of the nature of this project, retention of the concepts and skills will be extremely high and consistent. Students retain more information through the visual and applications mode of learning. We hope that teachers will find this project as exciting, inspiring, and exhilarating as the designer does.

Chapter Nine:
Using Writing to
Build Mathematical Power

by Sister Mary Megan Farrelly

Teachers who wish to foster mathematics achievement in their students will not overlook writing as a powerful tool for accomplishing that goal. Research by Janet Emig and others has proven that writing in the content areas facilitates the development of such skills as analyzing, interpreting, organizing, reasoning, synthesizing, evaluating, and internalizing. Additional research specifically in the field of mathematics (Nahrgang & Peterson, Bell & Bell, and others) has demonstrated that writing in this discipline has a positive influence on learning (Miller & England); however, teachers of mathematics have been slower to employ this technique with structure and regularity.

Although teachers who have integrated writing into mathematics instruction have done so in many creative ways, two general types of activities deserve special attention. These are learning logs and student journals. These two uses of writing have different objectives—learning logs focus on cognitive learning while student journals have communication as their purpose.

HOW TO TEACH MATH TO BLACK STUDENTS

Learning logs typically contain written responses to specific tasks, sometimes called writing prompts, assigned by the teacher. These students' writings may be definitions of mathematical terms expressed in the students' own words such as this explanation composed by a ninth grader who was asked to define triangles.

"Now I know that triangles are 180 degrees. I used to think they were 270 degrees. I know that every triangle has some different names. One on length of sides and one on angles" (McIntosh, 1991). The language may be imprecise, but the student indicates ownership of a concept previously not understood.

The following example illustrates another kind of learning log entry. It is a translation of mathematical process into English. The writing prompt given was: "Explain to a younger friend who must rely only on your written instructions how to factor a polynomial." Using 6b2+ 7b, the student writes:

"First find the number that could go into both the number 6 and 7. And there is no such number that goes into 6 or 7 so now go to the letter. Second find the letter that is lowest, and the letter is b because b2 is higher than b. subtract b from b2 and the answer is b, so put 6b next because 6b+b=6b2. Then put 7 because 7+b=7b, and work it out to check [the] problem" (Miller & England, 1989).

USING WRITING TO
BUILD MATHEMATICAL POWER

According to the student, $6b2+7b= b (6b+7)$, a correct solution. Without the student's accompanying text, the teacher would not realize that the student has a fundamental misperception about the nature of factoring, which could have an adverse effect on subsequent progress in mathematics. The student's text gives a clue to the teacher as to what re-teaching is needed in order for this student, and others, to understand that factoring is an operation of division not subtraction.

Learning log writing may be implemented by requiring that students write a brief explanation for each place they "get stuck" when trying to complete a homework assignment. It is uncommon for students to reflect in writing what they don't understand. Along similar lines, students may be asked, when it is appropriate, to write what one teacher calls a verification for a problem, i.e., a description of an alternative method for arriving at the same solution. Consider this problem and verification for simplifying an expression.

$72-3(5+8)$ This is the problem.

$72-3 \cdot 13$ I'm simplifying it now.

$72-39$ Now I'm doing order of operation(s).

33 Now I've arrived at the answer by subtraction.

72-3(5+8)   Here's the problem again.

72-(3x5) + (3x8)   I'm doing distribution now.

72-(15 + 24)   Now I work out the part in brackets and parentheses.

72-39= 33   Now I work out the problem. I subtract the number to get the answer.

These last two types of entries help students become independent learners. Verifications, in particular, bolster the students' self-confidence; in these writings, students must evaluate and confirm their own thinking. A variety of methods may be used to verify solutions, so verifications also have the capacity to develop the students' creativity.

Creativity can be stimulated too when students are asked to create their own word problems. This writing activity gives students the opportunity to make real-life connections to their learning and can be the catalyst for insightful and spirited cooperative learning sessions. Fifth graders authored these samples.

Barb: I "bought" a pack of bubble gum for $1.50. In the pack of gum, there are 10 "pieces" of gum. Each piece has 5 bubbles. How much does each bubble cost?

Using Writing to
Build Mathematical Power

Robbie: It is the year 1836. How many days until 1989? [His classmates let Robbie know that he needed information that is more precise in order to solve this problem!]

This last example is not a student-generated word problem, but the students' strategy for solving it demonstrates clear and accurate reasoning.

How many days old am I?

```
365      31      2
x11      -5      26
365      26      30
3650     31
4015     28
         31      223+4015= 4,238
         30      Mathematics is the key! $4238
        +16
         223
```

"To figure out how many days old I am, I first 'xed' 365 days (since that's how many days there are in a year) by my age. I am eleven years old. I came out with 4015. Then I added together all of the days from my birthday (October 5th) till now (May 16th). After adding the days, I came out with 223. Then I added 4015 to it. So the number of days I have had in my life is 4238. So now you know how many days old I am instead of years!" (Bresser & Sheffield).

To summarize, learning logs help each student participate in mathematics at a metacognitive level. Although learning logs are directed primarily at facilitating the students' progress in mathematics, it has been found that they help students acquire skill in writing as well as in mathematics.

Learning logs afford the teacher an opportunity to extend mathematics instruction beyond the time limitations of the mathematics class period. They give teachers a means of peeking into the students' thinking processes so they might better design future instruction. Learning logs make it possible for students to reflect on their own learning (and to learn in the act of reflection) and for teachers to nurture cognitive growth.

Whereas learning logs focus on the mental activity involved in learning, journal writing pertains more to students' attitudes and concerns, especially as they relate to mathematics. To initiate this type of writing, teachers may ask the students to complete open-ended sentences like these:

Something I do (don't) like about math is _____.

I think we do (don't) need to study math because _____.

An especially memorable math experience happened when ____.

Using Writing to
Build Mathematical Power

Teachers may assign writing prompts for journals too; they will simply have a different purpose. Teachers may solicit input from students on the content and pace of the course, on the learning activities and environment, and on their own self-assessment. Because student journals establish a line of communication between student and teacher, the key to their effectiveness lies in the teacher's ongoing response. Here are some journal entries that provided data helpful to the teacher for understanding and meeting students' feelings/needs.

"As a math student, I think the things we are doing now are really hard. At first it looked easy, but it isn't. I try to do the problems right, but somehow or other I end up with the wrong answer."

"I learn better when we work in groups. Other people are there to help you when you have trouble understanding. It makes you feel better."

"We are going too fast in class. We are constantly working, and if we don't take a break our heads are going to explode."

"What we are doing in algebra is frustrating. I don't like graphing much. It's too confusing for me to understand."

"I really don't like working in groups. I think a lot better working by myself...at my speed."

Writings in journals help the teacher get to know a lot about how the students feel about math and many other things (Steward and Chance).

The journal also gives the student a way to release tension and frustration. When students become accustomed to and comfortable with writing in journals, they feel free to ask questions they may be hesitant to bring up in class. The ever-important response to the teacher can do much to lessen the stress of mathematics anxiety, to recognize a student's effort in the face of difficulty, and to encourage the student to continue striving for success. It can be seen from the samples above that students' writings give the instructor clues as to what strategies (e.g., group or individual work, pacing of material) most benefit the learners. As the teacher utilizes this information to structure the course, a sense of partnership is created between the students and the teacher, a partnership that can only promote growth and learning.

Although learning logs and student journals have distinctly different objectives, it is not necessary to separate the two activities when using writing in mathematics instruction. If a teacher wishes, he/she may ask the students to keep notebook journals primarily for communicative writing, yet also ask the students to respond to cognitive-based prompts in their journals.

Conversely, students can write explanations and verifications as part of the assignment completed outside of class while in class they write personal reactions or

Using Writing to Build Mathematical Power

observations on those same papers before they are submitted to the instructor.

Returned papers can be kept in a portfolio so that each student has a record of his/her assignments and writings. Some instructors find it helpful to begin their classes with brief, timed writings about specific prompts; others like to conclude their classes that way, connecting the writing assignment to the class activity. Still others like to replace quizzes with learning log-type writings. The method of incorporating writing into mathematics instructions will vary from person to person. How one chooses to do this is not important. What is important is that writing be implemented with structure and regularity.

In its publication Curriculum and Evaluation Standards for School Mathematics, the National Council of Mathematics Teachers recommends instructional experience that will help students gain "mathematical power." The NCTM continues:

"This term denotes an individual's abilities to explore, conjecture, and reason logically as well as the ability to use a variety of mathematical methods effectively to solve routine problems. This notion is based on the recognition of mathematics as more than a collection of concepts and skills to be mastered....for each individual, mathematical power involves the development of personal self-confidence" (NCTM).

Too many students perceive mathematics as the memorization of rules and the mystical manipulation of symbols in pursuit of the right answer. When the rules are recited by rote but the processes are not understood and internalized, the right answer will continue to elude them. So too will the mathematical power necessary for an informed and productive life in an increasingly complex world. Implementing writing in mathematics instruction is a way to refocus on the skills that build mathematical muscle.

THE PROOF IS IN THE PUPIL

The following are excerpts from interviews of students I taught recently in a night school program at Lourdes High School in Chicago, Illinois.

It was a second semester Algebra I and II class. These students were previous Algebra I and Algebra II students who had failed the course at another school. The night school program offered students a way to make-up the class they failed. Most, if not all, of these students were labeled as slow or deficient learners. I offer these few excerpts and testimonials as evidence that the teaching strategies and approaches outlined in this book are effective and successful. The students were asked to evaluate the class, my teaching style, and previous math classes they had taken. Now lets hear from the students!

"I like how you taught me the simple way of Algebra. I like how you just broke things down in a simple way. The thing I liked most about this class was the great teacher I had to teach me. He was the first math teacher that I've ever really learned something from. He made everyone laugh, and he made class much more interesting. I hate school, but this teacher actually made me look forward to coming to school. Even though he talked a lot, everything he said made sense and I enjoyed every word of it."

"What I liked most about this class was that at the same time I learned more about math, it was fun and exciting."

"What I enjoyed most about this class was that the teacher really motivated everyone and let everyone know that what they have to say is important. I really do think that in this class I learned more than in other classes, and I also learned how to use what I've learned in the right way."

"It's fun and it isn't boring."

"You made us focus. Even when days seemed long, you always managed to keep our attention. You made learning fun, something worth doing. Not making students feel as if they have to, but making them feel as if they want to."

"Now it's simple because it's fun. You're always keeping our attention because you're always happy."

"You cared whether we learned or not."

"You were funny and at the same time you were teaching the lesson. I think that is important for the student."

"What I liked most was that our teacher was very understanding and one of the best teachers I've had."

"If I hadn't had a teacher with such energy, I probably would have failed again. If I had had a teacher like Mr. Muhammad, I would not have failed in the first place."

"I learned more in this classroom than in any other math class. I didn't used to care about my grades because I knew they were bad, but since you explained so much, I began to take interest. You compared problems to things we show interest in such as money, cars, etc., and you took math seriously but taught it in a leisurely way."

"I do feel more confident about my math skills. I don't think I love math, but I don't dislike it the way I used to."

"I feel more confident because my grades are higher and because he gave us confidence with his comments and lectures."

USING WRITING TO
BUILD MATHEMATICAL POWER

One hundred percent of the students indicated that they liked the class and thought that it was fun and exciting. Ninety-two percent indicated that they felt more confident about their math skills and had a greater appreciation for math after taking my class.

Ninety-eight percent of the students disliked their previous math classes either because of the teachers inability to explain or because the class was boring.

I would like to mention that the Lourdes High School Night School class that I taught was comprised mostly of inner-city Black and Hispanic students. There were 2 percent White, 38 percent Black, and 60 percent Hispanic students in the class.

Those of us who have decided to embark upon the perplexing mission of educating Black students must understand the seriousness and urgency of improving our current attempts and efforts. The educational system of this society has done and continues to do an extreme disservice to Black youth all across the country. The level of mathematical illiteracy among American students in general and Black students in particular is horrendous. If we desire to plan and map a course of resurrection, redemption, and restoration of the Black community as a whole, we must effect a complete revolution in the methodology and strategy that we are now using to teach mathematics.

HOW TO TEACH MATH TO BLACK STUDENTS

It is pertinent to the advancement of any nation to have a future generation that is mathematically and scientifically literate. Since Black people are on the bottom of the totem pole, we who care must make an even greater effort to increase the mathematical aptitude and proficiency of Black youth, for they are the ones who will participate in running the world. If a dramatic change is not made at once, we will continue to sentence countless generations of Black people to subordinate and underclass status and positions.

I believe we can turn this situation around through the improvement of mathematics education throughout the United States. There are many different educational theories and strategies that need to be studied and tested for their validity and reliability. In writing this book, I am in no way offering final or exclusive answers to the puzzle. Many scholars and educators have some very good strategies and methods that I use in conjunction with the methods offered in this book.

I believe that if my methods are utilized correctly and with the appropriate spirit, they will bring about a positive transformation in each classroom where they are applied. I offer these strategies and suggestions as a light and a guide through the dark and gloomy tunnel of today's educational system. I hope you find these "secrets of success" as beneficial and useful as I have and that we all can begin to make dramatic changes in the education and development of our children.

Chapter Ten:
Highway to Excellence in Mathematics:
Teaching College Mathematics to Culturally Diverse Students

According to the Office of Educational Research and Improvement,

> Minorities are not entering many important fields in mathematics and science. For example, Blacks make up 12 percent of the population, yet earn only 5 percent of the baccalaureate degrees awarded each year in science and mathematics, receive 1 percent of the Ph.Ds and make up only 2 percent of all employed scientists and engineers in the country. Hispanics make up 9 percent of the population, but represent only 3 percent of the baccalaureate degrees in science and mathematics, 2 percent of the Ph.Ds, and 2 percent of all employed scientists and engineers in the country.

Also, in a report put out only by the National Research Council it states that, "the under representation of this generation of minorities leads to further under representation in the next, yielding an unending cycle of mathematical poverty.

In a book entitled, *Minorities on Campus—A Handbook for Enhancing Diversity,* it states "Black and

Hispanic participation in graduate and professional education can best be described as miniscule in the areas mathematics and sciences. Only 462 Blacks earned doctorates in education, but only 6 in math and 8 in physics. Hispanics earned 12 in math and 15 in physics; American Indians earned one in math and none in physics.

It is evident from the above statistics that students from diverse backgrounds, mainly Blacks, Hispanics, and American Indians, are facing serious problems and difficulties in traditional college and university math classes. Throughout my years as a high school math instructor, I have encountered many students that have expressed instances where they have experienced difficulty in college or university math courses. Because of the tremendous number of people who have voiced their dissatisfactions and difficulties, I have been inspired to conduct an inquiry into this subject and discuss my findings and conclusions.

In a survey I constructed, on difficulties Black and Hispanic students encounter in traditional college math courses, 98% of the respondents state that they had problems in a college math course. Ninety-five percent indicated they had problems with the teaching style or methods of the professor.

In addition to the surveys, interviews were also conducted with several adult students and similar responses were given. The surveys and interviews all provided me with an enormous amount of information and insight into why so many of these students were experiencing difficulty in college math courses.

The following is a compilation of some of the areas of concern that came out of the survey responses and interviews:

Many students described the inability of the professor to explain and simplify the material as a major obstacle to their achieving and excelling in the math class. The participants pointed out that the professors spoke on a level that only mathematicians could understand and that they had no empathy nor concern for the student's ability to grasp the material.

There was a feeling on the students' part that their particular culture and history was not represented nor made mention of in the area of mathematics. There was a unanimous agreement that there was a void of the inclusion of the contributions of their people to the field of mathematics. They stated that this caused them to have low self-esteem, low self-confidence, and low self-worth.

Another overwhelming response that I extracted from the students, was the fact that the instructors rarely, if ever, made mention of the relevance of math to the real world. The students felt there was a lack of enthusiasm, inspiration, and motivation on the part of the instructor. The classes were perceived by many of the respondents as boring, unexciting, irrelevant and overall, a general waste of time.

Here is some quantitative data extracted from the responses to some of the survey questions:

21 out of 30 answered yes to the question, "Do you think your college math professor was or is difficult to understand?"

30 out of 30 answered No to the question, "Were the contributions of your people to the science of mathematics included in your college math class?"

16 out of 30 answered No to the question, "Did your math professor show concern for you learning the material?"

In a night school program that I instructed, there were 61% Hispanic students. All stressed a lack of inclusion of Hispanic contributions to the field of mathematics, in previous math courses they had taken.

29 out of 30 respondents answered No to the question, "Do you think the professor demonstrated and illustrated the relevancy of math to the real world?"

25 out of 30 of the respondents answered No to the question, "Did the professor inspire and motivate you to learn?"

27 out of 30 answered No to the question was your math class fun and exciting?"

These few statistics coupled with the many negative responses I got from interviewing people and observing students in math classes demonstrates clearly the dilemma that many students of diverse cultures are faced with when they enroll in college math courses. However, the quantitative data alone does not provide insight and depth into the seriousness of the problem. Therefore, I would like to offer some excerpts from the responses of the survey questions and interviews.

When asked to describe some of the problems the students had in previous college math courses, here is what some of the students stated:

"He really didn't explain well. Taught too fast. One time we had an exam and the exam was completely different from the study material. When asked about it the teacher laughed and said, "You thought the test was going to be that easy?"

"The teacher didn't use any manipulatives. There was no relevancy to the real world. There was no concern for the students. The instructor didn't even know you.

The class was boring and there was a lack of enthusiasm. It would have helped for the teacher to be motivating, inspiring and creative."

"He was very vague in explaining concepts. I took a course and passed it but I cannot remember anything from the class. There was no relevancy or practically. One instructor, all he did was repeat what was in the book. He did no explaining, no instruction. I passed because I regurgitated everything he gave me. He was arrogant. He had an I got mine you get yours' type of attitude."

"An instructor I had was so abstract and deep, he was on another plane. He was over the students' heads. He had no relevance or meaning to me."

"There was no concern. They did not spend a lot of time spoon-feeding. It was a do what I do, do what I say and you'll pass. It would have helped if they would have showed some concern, empathy. They had no personal skills, very cold."

"The instructor did not talk on the level of the Black and Hispanic students. We were made to feel inferior. We were put down, disgraced and he destroyed our self-esteem. Nine out of ten of the Black students failed and 3 out of 3 of the Hispanic students failed. The teacher said "This in not my problem, this is something you should know."

"There was too much theory. I never understood the concepts. The terminology was too abstract, full of jargon."

"The information being taught was irrelevant to my desire and motivations."

The participants in the surveys, and interviews were also asked to give recommendations on what could have been done to improve the math class and help them learn better. Here are some of the responses they gave:

"There was no use of manipulatives. We need to see and touch things. Black people are visual people. He could have used more projects. Grades should not always be based on test. He could have used other means of assessment. Also needs to use diverse teaching methods like computers, visuals, audio and applications."

"More independent drills, applications to the real world. Let students do problems as opposed to the teacher always. It would have helped a lot to have contributions of Blacks, creativity, different teaching techniques, more illustrations and visual presentations."

"Creativity, Applications, Empathy, Motivation, Concern, Care, and Inspiration."

"He could have explained the material in a manner that would have allowed me to relate it to self."

"He could have shown us how math is used in the real world, how and why math is important to us and had some practical, hands on activities."

"She could have made it more relevant to real world experience."

"Show a genuine concern. Show how to use the material in everyday life."

In a night school class, comprised of 2% White, 38% Black and 60% Hispanic students, 98% of the students stated that they disliked their previous math class, either because of the teacher's inability to explain or because the class was boring.

These few recommendations are extremely important to anyone concerned with fostering and promoting excellence amongst Black, Hispanic, and American Indian students. The excerpts and statistics bear witness to the urgent need to revitalize, transform and reform college and university math classes all across the country.

The views and perceptions of the adults I interviewed, observed and surveyed are not isolated and irrelevant opinions from a few disgruntled students. Much of what the students have shared and what I have heard and observed, can be validated, supported and confirmed by scholars and experts in the field of education. I would like to offer a few opinions and statements from scholars and research that are in direct accordance with the opinions and recommendations made by the respondents.

In a book by Marva Collins and Civia Tamarkin, *Marva Collins' Way,* the narrator, who observed Marva Collins' teaching methods, comments, she had an exuberance, an energy about her that was both captivating and contagious. It was Marva's attitude that made children learn. She was always convincing her students that there wasn't anything they could not do. Marva states, "A child who fidgets in his seat isn't necessarily hyperactive. Maybe that child is bored. A teacher can make or break a child, favor or stigmatize him. Just as there are teachers who are inspiring, who can spark interest and turn students on to learning, there are teachers who can turn a student off, not only to school but to himself."

These practical principles may be viewed by educators at the post secondary level as only applying to children, but it is my belief that this pedagogy can be useful at all grade levels. The comments and opinions of the students I talked with and surveyed, demonstrate the need for instructors to carry the same principles and methods that Marva Collins uses, into the college math class.

In a book *Minorities on Campus—A handbook for Enhancing Diversity,* strategies are outlined for the success of minorities in higher education. They state "Provide role models from minority racial and ethnic groups. Minority students need role models to motivate and inspire them to envision a future for themselves." They also go on to talk about biases of the professors. It states, "Professors unconscious assumptions that minority students are unable to perform up to par may become self-fulfilling prophecies. Or more subtle behaviors such as different treatment of minority students, dissimilar eye contact and other non-verbal behaviors may be equally negative for minority students." The book also points out that "many of our college courses are still primarily lectures, with students occupying a passive role in the learning process. Active involvement, frequent feedback and understanding of different ways of learning are some of the known ways to increase student learning."

A report entitled *Involvement in Learning and College: the Undergraduate Experience in America,* pointed to the following recommendations:

1) Frequent student-faculty contact in and out of classes is the most important factor in student motivation and involvement.

2) Students do not learn much just sitting in class listening to a teacher, memorizing prepackaged assignments and spitting out answers. They must talk about what they are learning, write about it, relate it to past experiences and apply it to their daily lives.

3) Expectations must be high. Respect diverse ways of learning. Be aware of assumptions you may have about minority students.

In the book *Helping Adults Learn* the ideal teacher of adults is:

> People-centered, more interested in individuality than conformity, more interested in finding solutions than in following rules. The teacher must have understanding, flexibility, patience, humor, practicality, creativity, and preparation.

It is also brought out in the book that,

> Learners who lack confidence in themselves are common. A good teacher needs to make the learning environment secure for everyone. Building their confidence is not condescending, but keeps their desire to learn alive. Enhancing security promotes learning.

Jacqueline Fleming points out in her book, *Blacks in College*, that

> On predominately black campuses, black students' successes are more likely to gain the attention of

107

faculty. Conversely, on White college campuses, Black students feelings of progress are thwarted. These students feel that instructors are not interested in them, do not give encouragement, and use unfair grading practices. Completed studies underscore the need for more Black faculty and staff members, a maximum of Black students with a balanced sex ratio, curricula relevant to the Black experience, and responsive counseling services.

In a detailed and practical study of the skills possessed by effective teachers and mentors in adult programs, Carol Schneider and her colleagues found that having positive expectations of students is one of the most important aspects of effective advising. Describing what their mentors did that was most helpful, students in my own research replied that they " Gave me confidence in myself," "kept pushing me and telling me I could do it," and "had faith in me even when I didn't" (Effective Teaching and Mentoring).

Angela Durante discovered in her dissertation entitled, "Importance of Peer Relations in Retention in College," that, "Students gravitate towards their own type and students gravitate toward teachers that are their own." This was indicated by her to be a strong finding in her study.

The Institute for the Learning Sciences published an article entitled, *Motivation in the Classroom*. In this article they state,

Children locked into classroom discussion are no different than adults locked into boring, irrelevant

HIGHWAY TO EXCELLENCE IN MATHEMATICS: TEACHING COLLEGE MATHEMATICS TO CULTURALLY DIVERSE STUDENTS

meetings. If you do not understand how something relates to your goals, you will not care about that thing because we do not want our children to be motivated solely by a desire to please the teacher, what we need to address is how to make the content of the curriculum fit into the concerns of the child. If a piece of content addresses a particular concern of a student, or even a general area of interest, that student will not tune it out.

Lastly, in the book *Multiple Intelligence Approaches to Assessment*, Howard Gardner outlines seven ways of knowing. Each of the seven multiple intelligences demands a different method of planning lessons and assessing students in math class, that involve creativity and a sensitivity to the diverse ways of knowing students come to a math class with. This book sheds light on the need for instructors to provide a variety of teaching methods and strategies. The author categorized the seven ways of knowing as the follow:

Verbal/ Linguistic
Logical/ Mathematical
Visual/ Spatial
Body/ Kinesthetic
Musical/ Rhythmic
Interpersonal
Intrapersonal

After analyzing and studying the recommendations and suggestions of scholars, educators and researchers and

109

incorporating and integrating them with those of the adult students, I have developed guidelines, strategies and methodologies that synthesize the principles and themes of everyone. As we embark upon the mission of uplifting, resurrecting and revitalizing the mathematics instruction of minorities at the post secondary level, it is crucial for us to be aware of the opinions of our students as well as those experts in the field. I would like to propose the following guidebook as just one step toward this effort.

The instructor must value each student's concerns and possess a general concern for the students' well being.

The instructor must demonstrate a desire to see all students excel and succeed.

The instructor must nurture and cultivate students' self-confidence and self-esteem.

Each student must be fed positivity and made to believe that they can achieve and excel.

Minority students must have some minority staff and faculty members in the math department that they can identify and relate to.

Instructors must incorporate and integrate the contributions of each student's cultural background to the science of mathematics.

Instructors must be sensitive to and cognizant of displaying verbal or nonverbal suggestions of racist discriminatory practices and treatment.

Highway to Excellence in Mathematics: Teaching College Mathematics to Culturally Diverse Students

Instructors must treat all students with equity, fairness and justice.

Instructors must make themselves accessible, available and approachable to all students.

The college math class must become alive, vibrant and enthusiastic.

Instructors must be motivated, inspiring, animated, and creative.

The college math class must incorporate a variety of teaching methods, strategies and techniques.

Each students' diverse learning style and way of knowing must be recognized and respected by instructors.

Instructors must do more teaching than lecturing. Each class should be student centered.

Instructor must use a variety of assessment tools and devices.

Instructors must incorporate the use of practical and real world applications in the math courses.

Instructors must demonstrate how the math content is relevant to the experiences and realities of each student.

Instructors must master the ability to break material down into pieces that each student can digest.

Students must become more involved and active in the math class.

The instructor must have patience, flexibility, humor, practicality and understanding.

Instructors must have high expectations for each student and communicate them to the student's on a regular basis.

Instructors must master the art of questioning to probe students' minds and to obtain crucial and vital understanding and mastery.

There must be a dramatic improvement in the amount of and quality of student-faculty interaction.

Students of color need to see role models who have mastered and excelled in math.

The instructor should incorporate and integrate the use of manipulatives, visuals, computer simulations, videos, audios, models and other technology.

Now I will provide further areas of recommendation with a more in depth discussion for the instructor.

Build Confidence and Faith

A general theme that permeated the discussions by the students on the problems they had with previous instructors was the lack of concern and care for the students' success. Many students stressed that the teacher cared less if the students' grasped the material and some even identified negative comments and body language that was given off by the teacher.

Most if not all of use are familiar with the self-fulfilling prophecy. Students' confidence and faith in themselves, many times, is shaped and molded by the reactions and stimuli that they pick up from the instructor. This was pointed out clearly by Chickering and Ganson in an article entitled "Seven Principles for Good Practice in Undergraduate Education Wingspread Journal." They state that "Good practice communicates high expectations. High expectations are important for everyone—for the poorly prepared, for those unwilling to exert themselves and for the bright and well-motivated."

We, as instructors, even at the post secondary level must provide verbal as well as nonverbal communication that transmits positivity and high expectations. College students need a sense of belonging and confidence just as much as primary or secondary level students. Especially for Black and Hispanic students who most of the time evolve out of negative mathematical experiences and backgrounds. The Black and Hispanic student needs to feel a sense of confidence in themselves and an attitude that says that I can achieve and master this.

From *Minorities on campus—A Handbook for Enhancing Diversity,* the author states,

> Colleges and universities can expect to have their minority students graduate if they expect all students to achieve and provide counseling and support programs. Professors' unconscious assumptions that minority students are unable to perform up to par may become self-fulfilling prophecies.

Also from a book entitled, *Helping Adults Learn,* William Draves, the author points out that "Learners who lack confidence in themselves are common in adult learning. Building their confidence is not condescending, but keeps their desire to learn alive."

Being confident in one's ability is paramount to excellence in performance. Any individual who lacks confidence and faith in themselves will find it extremely difficult to channel their willpower to accomplish what they desire.

Black and Hispanic student's suffer greatly from this predicament because many lack confidence in themselves especially as it pertains to dexterity in math and science. There exists an unwritten law in this society that states that Black and Hispanics are inferior and less intelligent. This unwritten law has affected the attitudes of Black and Hispanic students to the point where they have fabricated a belief of inferiority that impedes their ability to learn to excel in math.

College math instructors can provide instruction and teaching that destroys the inferiority complex that these students possess which in turn will regenerate and revitalize the students' spirit and will to learn. The appropriate classroom environment and methodology can serve to refine and nurture the students' assurance in themselves.

Assessment

If we are to reform the teaching of math at the post secondary level, we cannot by pass the importance of interactions between student and teacher. One of the most important aspects of this interaction is in the area of assessment.

Assessment is the gathering of information for decision-making. It is one of the most critical areas to be studied if the interaction between teacher and student is to be meaningful. Assessment helps the teacher determine the magnitude of understanding and comprehension of the mathematical ideas expressed in the classroom, in order for changes or modifications to be made for the betterment of the students.

This area has to be of the utmost priority to us as educators, for this is the means by which we determine whether our transmission of mathematical data and information has been received. When someone sends a fax or sends a package, they are concerned with whether the message or package was received. If assessment is not viewed seriously, than we are missing a very crucial aspect of teaching.

We can see by studying the research on the mathematical literacy of Black and Hispanic students in particular, that dramatic change must take place in the areas of assessment.

As rapid changes take place in the science of mathematics, so is the conception of assessment also changing. No longer can college math professors justify assessing and evaluating students through paper and pencil methods. The scope and aim of assessment must mature to a much more wholistic stage, where many methods and instruments will be used to ascertain an individual's knowledge of math.

Not all students possess the ability to display learning through the quiz and test mode. Nevertheless, unfortunately at the post secondary level, most professors evaluate and assess students by this method. They simply give a quiz, a midterm and a final. This is not an adequate nor a justifiable method of assessment. Some students can express themselves better through oral, visual or kinesthetic modes. In addition, the written test or quiz usually only assesses the student's grasp of rote knowledge and does not delve deeper into different levels of learning.

There are a wide range of areas and abilities that a math professor can assess. Students should be assessed on their use of math strategies and skills, their understanding of concepts, principles and rules, their attitude and feelings toward math, their problem solving and critical thinking skills and their perception of the real world applications of math. The list can go on since there exists a variety of learning goals and objectives when it comes to ascertaining mastery and competency of mathematics. When the college math professor begins to vary and experiment with different assessment methods and tools, this allows those students who are not good test-takers an avenue to display their comprehension and learning in a different mode, thereby increasing their chances of excelling and moving on to the next level.

Highway to Excellence in Mathematics: Teaching College Mathematics to Culturally Diverse Students

Here are just a few methods and techniques that professors can implement in the classroom to improve our assessment:

1) Assessment should not occur always at the end of a lesson or in the middle of a term. The assessment should be an integral part of the instruction. Provide learning activities and experiences that permit you to do an assessment as the students are learning.

2) Use a variety of methods and instruments to assess your students.

   Examples:
   a) have students write or verbalize problem solving methods, steps and strategies.
   b) have students give audio-visual presentations about what they learned.
   c) have students develop songs, poems, stories, cartoons or rhymes on some math concept, principal or skill.
   d) have students play the role of the instructor and explain the lesson to the rest of the class.
   e) have students get involved in collaborative and cooperative learning activities.

f) have students write and develop their own problems.

g) have students use technology to explain a concept, rule or principle. Computers, overhead projectors, video, and audio, filmstrips, tapes, etc.

Since the science of mathematics is so complex and intricate, the assessment of the student cannot be limited to one method. How can we see the various definitions of what mathematics is by different mathematicians, who describe the broadness and magnitude of math, yet place a limit on the methods by which we assess its understanding. If one can describe math as being as vast and infinite as the universe, than should not we view assessment of students' knowledge of math as being diverse and multidimensional?

Self Identity and Self-Esteem

In Cassava and Silverman's book, *Maximizing Student Potential,* they point out "the learner behaves in ways which are related to self-concept and self efficacy beliefs. Self-concept can become a self-fulfilling prophecy as a person tends to behave in ways that are consistent with it. Gross underestimates of academic ability may have a negative impact on academic performance."

Highway to Excellence in Mathematics: Teaching College Mathematics to Culturally Diverse Students

This is the dilemma that the college math professor may face when dealing with Black and Hispanic students, who have a tendency to underestimate their math abilities and potential due to negative math histories.

Society has not helped Black and Hispanic students develop a positive self-concept and self-efficacy beliefs about their math ability. They are usually placed in low-level math classes in the public and private school systems, which label them as slow or underachievers. Not only are they relegated and placed in slow math courses and viewed as being underachievers and at-risk students, but they also suffer from a lack of self-confidence and self-esteem as it relates to performance in the math class. This can stem from a lack of representation and identification of self with the math content.

Another very prevalent problem with many college math students is the fact that they are not taught the universality of math. They are not given enough real-world applications that would illustrate to them how math is connected to every aspect of life.

The Math Class Must Come Alive

The survey that I took of college students on how they felt about their math classes indicated that many students believe and feel that their math courses were boring and irrelevant. We cannot expect optimum performance from our students if they are bored, unmotivated and uninspired.

Unfortunately, this is the prevailing feeling of most students enrolled in college math courses.

Most college math courses are teacher-centered and utilize an expository teaching style. Professors are usually found lecturing to the students and dominating the learning atmosphere and activity. Some students are used to this type of teaching style and can survive long enough to excel and move to the next level. However, many students, particularly Black and Hispanic, have a great deal of difficulty with this boring approach to teaching.

As professors, we cannot simply lecture to students and expect them to garner some motivation and inspiration out of nowhere.

The college math class must not be simply teacher-centered. It must evolve to become a student-centered and an investigative-oriented classroom. Students should be found exploring, discovering, problem solving, analyzing and experimenting with various math concepts, and principles and skills. When the students are an intricate part of the learning environment, they are much more excited and motivated to learn.

According to Chickering and Ganson

Good practice encourages active learning. Learning is not a spectator sport. Students do not learn much just sitting in classes listening to teachers, memorizing prepackaged assignments and spitting out answers. They must talk about what they are learning, write about it, relate it to past experience and apply it to their daily lives.

HIGHWAY TO EXCELLENCE IN MATHEMATICS: TEACHING COLLEGE MATHEMATICS TO CULTURALLY DIVERSE STUDENTS

College math professors must make dramatic changes in this area. Most math professors are concerned only with how accurately and how rapidly students can compute arithmetic operations, simplify algebraic expressions, or integrate an expression. We are producing calculators and robots in our students. We cannot continue down this boring path of math instruction if we truly desire well-educated math students.

How can we bring the math class to life? How can we foster interest, motivation and vibrancy into the math class?

1. We must instruct the student in a manner that the relevance and validity for every mathematical rule, law or skill is clearly defined and understood. Students must not only know the information but be able to articulate why it works the way it does and be able to provide the students with a deeper understanding and a greater appreciation for math. One of the greatest and most pertinent questions that can be asked is why. Students are neither comfortable, nor are they satisfied with learning an enormous array of facts, theorems, rules and shortcuts, which are void of rationale, validity and proof.

2. We must instruct students on when to use a rule, skill or law in math. Many students learn the basic arithmetic operations, but because they do not

learn when to use them, they cannot solve real world problems or applications involving them.

3. An excellent method of fostering critical thinking and reasoning skills, while creating a learning environment bubbling with fun and excitement, is to integrate the use of games and puzzles into the instructional activities. Students become caught up with the fun and excitement of the games, and they forget that they do not like math or have a fear of math.

4. There are many math games that can be found in books, periodicals, or computer software. I would also recommend that the instructor develop and design games of his/her own.

5. Another way to bring life to the math class is to implement the use of brainteasers and puzzles. This serves to inspire and motivate the students through challenging them and using a mode of learning that is different and exciting.

I have found that the gifted as well as slow learners enjoy being mentally challenged and it provides for a fun and interesting learning atmosphere.

Using brainteasers and puzzles in the math class provide development in many areas of the mind that are necessary to advance to higher, more complex sciences and math. Some areas that can be enhanced and developed are critical thinking skills, reasoning abilities, visualization and perception skills and problem solving.

There are many different types of brainteasers and puzzles. Many can be found in books, periodicals or through educational product distributors.

6. Lastly, since most Black and Hispanic students are fascinated and captured by music, videos, movies and television, the math professor must incorporate different modes of learning into the classroom, as to harness some of this energy and interest.

This can be achieved by using a diverse range of modalities when teaching. We should all be familiar with the various differences in learning styles that students possess. It is incumbent upon the professor to vary the types of sense modalities they utilize in the math instruction.

Professors can utilize the visual sense by providing charts, graphs, tables, diagrams, films, videos, posters, computer simulations and overhead transparencies. This will help students better retain the concepts and will stimulate more interest and a desire to learn.

The auditory sense can be stimulated through the professors use of audiotapes, music, songs, rhymes, poems and oral presentations.

Professors should also utilize the sense of touch by providing hands-on activities, manipulatives, experiments and constructive projects and models. When students are provided instruction using various sense modalities they are more apt to grasp math concepts deeper and retain them longer. The stranger and more unorthodox the teaching method, the more it will be retained.

There are more increasing numbers of students entering college under prepared and underdeveloped. Therefore, it is incumbent upon all those who care to develop strategies, techniques and programs that will serve to provide assistance and aid where needed.

CHAPTER ELEVEN: PUTTING THE PIECES TOGETHER

*"The Journey of a Thousand Miles Begins
With the First Step!" Confucious*

The above quote sheds light on the perplexity and complexity of the scope of the mission to raise the mathematical competency and achievement of African-American students. Many scholars have approached the problem from various angles, philosophies and positions. What must be understood by all is the fact that anyone trying to pinpoint the problem to one specific variable has not thoroughly researched or analyzed the current dilemma facing African-American students. Those that desire to embark upon this journey must come to understand the magnitude of it and that this journey is likened to a journey of a thousand miles.

There are numerous statistics, figures and studies that exist, which confirms the devastating condition of the African-American student in relation to their persistence and achievement in mathematics and science. One only needs to type in African-American performance in math and science into the computer to see the enormous amount of studies and research documenting the low performance of our students. If we were to analyze this condition as a physician, we would be mind -boggled at the intricate multi-varied nature of the problem.

The African-American condition is unique to any other ethnic group or people on the Planet Earth. Centuries of oppression, racism, discrimination and self-destructive habits all combine to form a cycle of impediments that serve to add injury to injury. The situation for Blacks in America and throughout the world in the area of education is synonymous with a "Catch 22". Numerous negative factors come together to magnify the sickness, making a common cold become a cancer.

Any scholar who believes there is a genetic or biological deficiency amongst Blacks that makes them predetermined to fail in the areas of math and science, is functioning from a racist immature mentality that blinds them to the realities Blacks face everyday. Unfortunately, many of these scholars and researchers get credit and validation from educational institutions and administrators who design curriculum and programs, which serve to compound the problem. The African American student therefore suffers in the long- run because their needs are not being met because those in charge do not have the proper knowledge to address the serious and vital issues that affect our youth.

One educator, Eleanor Orr, makes a similar argument in her book, *Twice as Less"* where she states:

Tragically, as the debate over such issues goes on, disproportionate numbers of young blacks continue to be labeled," handicapped", "learning disabled", or "behavior problems". And many educators, instead of paying attention to documented language differences that may be interfering with performance of these students in school, continue to think in terms of cultural deprivation and compensatory education.

She continues in a later paragraph:

As everyone well knows, such disproportionate distribution is justified by some with the claim that blacks are genetically less intelligent than whites, and is explained by others as reflecting a raft of supposed deficiencies in the home environment of black children. The focus is still on deficiencies rarely simply on differences that may be interfering with performance.

I fully concur with Orr's comments. It is much easier for these scholars and educators, who think and perceive that blacks suffer from deficiencies as opposed to differences, to argue in this manner, because it frees the society, the educational system and educators from any need to transform or reform. The blaming the victim syndrome is a slick way of escaping providing the funding, programs and training needed to adequately meet the needs of a population that is deemed unimportant and insignificant by those in authority and power.

HOW TO TEACH MATH TO BLACK STUDENTS

It is a blessing that we do have a growing number of educators and scholars who are not falling into the blaming the victim syndrome and are broadening their scope of analysis to find the real stumbling- blocks that African-American students are facing. One such educator, that I mentioned above, Eleanor Orr, has a very unique and pertinent outlook on one of the variables that serves to sentence our students to low performance and achievement in math and science. Orr identifies one of the problems as so:

"In this book I show how the misunderstanding that had puzzled me relate to the students nonstandard uses of certain prepositions and conjunctions that in standard English distinguish certain quantitative ideas, and I show why there is reason to believe that these nonstandard uses are rooted in the grammar of Black English Vernacular (BEV). I emphasize, however, that it is the many similarities between BEV and standard English that make the differences a problem-more of a problem than they would be if the vocabularies and grammars of the languages were totally distinct."

"Many African American students confuse half and twice. From a mathematical perspective, they are opposites. One half of 10 is different from 10 twice any number. Twice as less is performing multiplication and subtraction simultaneously. This explains why many African American youth have math challenges, particularly with word problems."

As a teacher of mathematics for 14 years, I have come across students who misunderstand instructions, directions and math concepts simply out of a misunderstanding of mathematical vocabulary and how they translate in their everyday language. This is why I try to stress the importance of mastering the ability to translate mathematical concepts and terms into the English language. I also attempt to use the student's backgrounds and unique language or Black English Vernacular, to integrate it into a framework where it is easily comprehensible. One of the successes of any math teacher lies in their ability to break down the symbolic abstractness of mathematics into simplistic and real meaningful dialogues for the students. There is a saying amongst the hip-hop artists to keep it real. This is precisely what the math teacher must do in order to attract the minds of black youth to mathematical knowledge. One educator does a marvelous job, with his program and project, The Algebra Project, of keeping the mathematics real for the student. Educator Robert P. Moses speaks about his project and curriculum in his book, *Radical Equations,* where he states:

> Our transition curriculum is rooted in the conviction that intellectual development is in part, a matter of integrating knowledge. You want the kids to learn how to engage the inquiry process, In other words, in the Algebra Project we are using a version of experiential learning: it starts with where the children are, experiences they share. We get them to reflect on these drawing on their common culture, then to form abstract conceptualizations out of their reflection, and then to apply the abstraction back on their experience.

HOW TO TEACH MATH TO BLACK STUDENTS

The success of the Algebra Project demonstrates how African American students can achieve when proper and appropriate teaching strategies are utilized. Most mathematics curriculums do not incorporate the interests and culture of African-American students in a mode that inspires and motivates them to learn. I see the definition of a good teacher as one who can disseminate knowledge in such a manner that the student can integrate the new knowledge with their past and present experiences to produce a harmony and synthesis that evolves the student from where they are to new stages of development. Teachers of mathematics have the tremendous task of demonstrating and illustrating to students that mathematics plays an integral role and part in their everyday reality. Students must see a connection between their individual world and the world of mathematics. Mr. Moses makes this point clear in his book. He states:

> In the Algebra Project this movement from experience to abstraction takes the form of a five-step process that introduces students to the idea that many important concepts of elementary algebra can be accessed through ordinary experiences. Each step is designed to help students bridge the transition from real life. The transition curriculum is not only experiential, but culturally based. The experiences must be meaningful in terms of the daily life and culture of the students.

This is key when it comes to educating the African-American student. There is a saying that most Black students learn more from what they see and touch, then from what they hear. If educators are not making the mathematics real, by designing activities, programs and lessons, which incorporate hands-on and visual, then the African-American student finds it difficult to relate the abstractness and ambiguity of the math curriculum to the reality of the world in which they live. There are many teachers of mathematics, who have an understanding of the mathematics, but cannot transmit their understanding in such a manner that they can convey it to others. Mr. Moses makes an excellent point in relation to this. He comments:

> There are a lot of well-trained curriculum experts and others who know a great deal about math, but, I began to tell myself, what is missing from their work is insight into the minds of the young people they are trying to reach. We do not have enough people with a solid enough mastery of math who are so guided by their insights into the student's way of thinking they can reconceptualize the math in terms that allow their students to connect. In fact, the culture moves people in the opposite direction. As you become more and more accomplished in the math, you become more and more distant from the younger students.

I have found that when I structure my mathematics instruction to include projects, experiments, demonstrations, simulations and exhibitions, the students were highly motivated and interested in learning. They also seemed to retain more of the knowledge and concepts.

Especially in the early grades, our children want to see, feel, touch and experience the liveliness of mathematics. The mathematics classroom should enable students to take the knowledge and produce something tangible that will be a concrete representation of what they learned. The beauty of the Algebra Project can be found in their five-steps that make up the curriculum process. One step of the process that I found very interesting involves the use of physical events where students take trips and excursions to familiar places to research and study some mathematical principle or concept. The second step is vital also because it allows students to draw a picture or construct a model of the event they experienced or studied on the trip. This brings the math class out of a boring textbook or lecture by the instructor, into the realm of the student's environment and enables them to place meaning and value on the learning.

I applaud the work of both Eleanor Orr and Robert Moses. I believe they have made great contributions to the mission to understand what explains the low performance, persistence and achievement of Black students in mathematics. In addition to these two educator's contributions and perspectives, there is an educator named Danny Martin, whose multiple-varied outlook and perspective fit firmly into my philosophy of the reasons for this low performance amongst African-Americans. In his book, *Mathematics Success and Failure Among African-American Youth,* he looks at mathematical performance from a social perspective and one of multiple factors and variables. He introduces a concept he calls, "mathematics identity". I strongly believe that this concept has great significance and relevancy to our discussion of what are some of the causes of the low performance. He defines mathematics identity in these words:

> Mathematics identity- one's belief about his or her mathematics abilities, one's beliefs about the instrumental importance of mathematics, one's beliefs about opportunities and constraints that exist to participate in mathematics, and one's motivation to obtain mathematics knowledge.

This multi-varied outlook on the situation made much sense to me, since much of what I see as the cause of some of the negative statistics we see amongst African-American students in mathematics is not necessarily a cognitive deficiency but more of a lack of inspiration, motivation, dedication and self-confidence. What I see, are outside forces that destroy inner drives and confidence to overcome the difficulties inherent in studying a discipline such as mathematics. Many of the successes I have witnessed over the years have come from my ability to utilize the appropriate motivational and inspirational methods and tools that caused students to value, appreciate and enjoy learning mathematics. In my teaching methodology, I attempt to destroy the perspective of math as irrelevant and insignificant by integrating student's interests into the math curriculum to allow students to see the relationship between what they experience in the real world with the mathematics they experience in my classroom.

In reading Mr. Martin's writings on the subject, I notice his words were congruent with my thoughts. According to Martin:

> The dispositions and behaviors that I observed among students at Hillside were not due to students ability, content difficulty or biased curriculum. Most students, when given support and direction, could exhibit the kind of mathematical understanding that the teachers expected. Also, the students were working with a curriculum that was specifically designed to take advantage of their real-world experiences and to make mathematics more meaningful to them.

This is part of the journey that many teachers of mathematics do not seem to want to undertake, because it requires them to come out of the traditional mode of teaching and come out of their comfort zones. The success I have had in my classroom, the success that Orr, Moses and Martin have written about, all requires creativity, hard-work, innovation and dedication that many educators do not feel the need, nor the desire to devote the necessary energy and time to. Therefore, the question we must as educators ask is, "Do we really want progress and success amongst our students?" If the answer is yes, than we must take the first step and began to put all the pieces to the puzzle together.

Another aspect of this first step is to look more closely at the research Danny Martin outlines in his book. When addressing his concept of mathematics identity, he articulates an aspect of his perspective of the problem as such:

> In my view, the most significant aspect of examining cultural and community beliefs about mathematics is being able to identify and counter those beliefs about mathematics that have a potentially negative effect on African-American children. It is not difficult to imagine that where negative messages do exist, they have a historical basis and will probably be reflected in parents and community members' accounts of their own negative experiences in mathematics-related contexts, rationalizations about their own lack of success in mathematics, and conflicts with teachers and school officials.

He continues,

> One consequence of these kinds of community beliefs is that African-American children might respond by disassociating themselves from the doing of mathematics as an instrumental endeavor when it appears that doing mathematics is for others.

These comments by Martin are very supportive of my viewpoint, that much of the low levels of persistence and achievement can be traced to negative attitudes and perceptions about mathematics and their abilities to understand and master it. Many of us are familiar with the saying; Your Attitude Affects Your Altitude. The student's will is directed by his or her desire to accomplish what they set their minds to. Desire is fed by the attitude of the individual. Mr. Martin's comments and research illustrates that African-American students attitudes and perceptions of the relevance and importance of mathematics is predicated upon their beliefs, their parent's beliefs and the beliefs of community members. I strongly believe that the student's beliefs are molded and fashioned by their attitudes towards that which they are engaged in. The "mathematics identity" concept that Martin introduced bears witness to the fact that if the African-American student's perception and attitude is negative towards mathematics, this will have a damaging effect on their performance, persistence and achievement. This fact should shed light on those scholars and researchers who narrow their focus to discussions on deficiencies, shortcomings and deprivations. I am not stating that these factors don't play some role in the problems, but they should not be singled out and given the most attention. We must broaden our scope and began to take into consideration seriously the effect of sociocultural, socioeconomic and community concerns.

Putting the Pieces Together

We must ask questions like: What is the attitude of most black students towards mathematics? What is the attitude of most parents and members of the black community towards mathematics? Those of us who have a hand on the pulse of the black community and reality know that it is rare to find a discussion on the relevance and importance of being mathematically literate and competent. Most black children are not exposed to stimuli, whether visual or auditory, that inspires and motivates them to want to learn math. If we analyze all of the modes of influence on the minds of black children and black people in general, there are hardly any that guides us to construct a positive outlook and attitude towards math.

In Martin's research, he conducted interviews on parents and students. Most of them expressed negative histories, experiences and perceptions of mathematical relevancy and value. Many spoke of their dislike for math and how their parents, friends and relatives all disliked and performed below average in math. Now go back to my earlier comments on the effects of attitude on desire and will. If most African-Americans possess a negative attitude and perception of math, what do we expect their desire to learn and be proficient at it to be?

Mr. Martin addresses this in these words:

> One of the most fruitful aspects of studying these community beliefs about mathematics is showing that the legacy of denied opportunity and differential treatment in mathematics contexts is a

potent and viable factor that operates to inform and affect the day-to-day lives of many African-American adults. Then knowledge of and responses to the legacy influences their perceptions of themselves, their beliefs about their capabilities as parents, and their expectations for their children. These community beliefs about mathematics contribute to the context that students look to for messages about the importance of mathematics and may represent the most important link in building sufficiently complex explanations for mathematics achievement and persistence among black students.

These statements by Martin raise my confidence and hope that the journey of a thousand miles can be realized and reached. If attitude, motivation and perception are part of the problem than there is hope for improvement and change, since these factors are all temporal and transformable. As an educator I have witnessed students with very negative attitudes and low self-confidence transform these feelings through proper utilization of methods and strategies that serve to instill confidence, appreciation and motivation into the student's mental framework. Listen to the words of one of the parents that Martin interviewed in his research:

Sarah: Because, like I said, I don't think they think it matters. It's like, "Why do I have to take this math class? I'm not going to use it. I don't think they think it really matters. But it does. I see now that it does. But then I did not think it really mattered. I think they get the attitude," I don't want to do this" So, they do it to get a grade and that's it. I believe that's why because they don't think it matters. They don't think they're going to use it later in life.

Imagine if some teacher, parent or community member could have reached Sarah earlier and changed her outlook and perception of math from negative to positive. This, in my judgment, is a vital component missing in most approaches to the problem. We must find innovative and revolutionary methods, strategies and programs that will serve to create positive attitudes and beliefs about mathematics amongst members of the African-American community. I suggest we launch an all out campaign starting in the earlier grades and even preschool, to bombard our children with knowledge, information and stimuli that will allow them to see the relevance and necessity of being a mathematically literate member of society. Career days, workshops and seminars could be set up in the African-American communities to educate both children and adults on the critical relationship between success in today's technologically expanding world and being mathematically competent and proficient. Just as we see various literacy campaigns, advertisements and special programs to inspire people to read, we must now utilize the same amount of energy and resources to promote mathematical literacy.

The success of this campaign is predicated upon a holistic approach. We cannot launch a campaign with just a few individuals who see this as relevant and vital for our community and nation. Listen at the comments of Mr. Moses from his book, *Radical Equations*, on this note. He states:

> Yet the literacy effort really cannot succeed unless it enlists the active participation of some critical mass of the mathematical community. The question of how we all learn to work across several arenas is unsolved. Those arenas are large and complicated. They include the curriculum itself, instructional philosophy, schools, school systems, and individual classrooms. Communities and their process of social change must also be centrally involved, and in some broad sense, national and local politics. Really working in all these arenas will require that many people adopt a more holistic outlook than they have ever done before.

As the old African saying goes, it takes a village to raise a child; it will take every avenue available in the Black community to take the necessary steps to make this effort successful. The social, religious, educational and political institutions that effect black people must all view this current dilemma as a state of emergency. Just as the ability to read is seen as a national necessity, being mathematically competent and proficient must also be given the same concern and attention.

As we launch this campaign and mission, we should not overlook utilizing the modes of influence that predominates the minds of our youth. I strongly believe if we can utilize the television, the music industry, video games, computers and the sport and entertainment world, as a means to send messages to our youth about the importance of mathematics, this will have a great impact on erasing the negative attitudes and perceptions our youth possess. Think about our youth turning on the television and viewing a program or commercial that speaks to how math is used in different aspects of our lives. What if we could get basketball, baseball and football stars to speak about how they use math in their sport, or what if some of the popular rappers could rap about the importance of learning math? Suppose we could create video games, which teach mathematical concepts and skills? How about billboards and posters on buses, in train stations and throughout the major cities that instruct our youth to master math? Just as there is numerous liquor, cigarette and gym shoe advertisements in the ghettoes, why can't we advertise the need to be mathematically literate? It can happen if we all get on board. This can be a reality. Mr. Robert Moses spoke in his book about how the civil rights movement started out as a tiny thought in someone's mind and then later spread from house to house, block to block, community to community and eventually state to state.

One program that encompasses the commitment and holistic approach I have been writing about is a nonprofit program called, "Project Seed." "It is an organization of mathematicians and scientists from industry, universities and research corporations who Socratically teach advanced, conceptually oriented mathematics to at-risk students in urban areas." I strongly support and admire this program because it involves all the components of education: the student, parents, teachers and community members. Project Seed has a long history of miraculous success in teaching higher mathematics and critical thinking skills to so-called at-risk students. Their success lies in their concentrated focus on developing the student, the teaching staff as well as the families of the students. The program combines classroom instruction, professional development, an advanced mathematics curriculum and family involvement.

The classroom teachers are supported with math specialists that model the correct instructional methodology, which helps to avoid any misunderstandings or misuses of the methodology. The teachers are not just given modeling, but they are also equipped with numerous resources and training that enhances their instructional skills and techniques. According to the Project Seed description, "In addition to modeling in the classroom, teachers participating in the professional development program attend staff development workshops discussing various aspects of the Project Seed Socratic group discovery methodology and of Project Seed's advanced math curriculum. The program works hard to develop superb teachers by supporting them with all the necessary training, development and pedagogy needed to nurture their growth and evolution."

Not only are the teachers in Project Seed nurtured and enriched constantly to bring out the best in them, but the program utilizes a unique combination of questioning, interaction and Socratic discovery techniques that creates an exciting learning environment. They believe in the Socratic style and intellectual challenges stimulate students. This is easy to see in the students as they actively participate in the classroom, as they confidently tackle advanced conceptual mathematics, and even as they use their creativity and enthusiasm to express their feelings about Project Seed in skits, songs and dances at Seed family events such as a Project Seed Gala or a demonstration at a parent-teacher meeting." This is the type of learning environment and atmosphere that is missing in most math classrooms across the country. I love the interactive discovery aspect of Project Seed's approach, along with their use of family events, where students can express their mathematical understanding and appreciation using a variety of sense modalities. Many schools have talent shows and art shows, but Project Seed's math demonstrations and events are rare finds in most schools today.

The Project Seed techniques have proven to get results. This supports my belief that in the right environment and atmosphere for learning, our students can aspire to greatness and manifest their God-given talents and skills. Listen to what Project Seed says about the environment their techniques create": These techniques along with Socratic interactive questioning and a carefully planned flow of mathematics, combine to create an environment that provides opportunities for all students to have success, and intellectual FUN!"

Lastly, Project Seed works hard to overcome one of the great obstacles to teaching African-American students and that is gaining the support, involvement and participation of the student's parents and family members. Project Seed has, as one of their four main components, a department dedicated to family involvement. This is a vital component in solving the problem of low performance and achievement amongst our students. We must work hard to gain the support of family and community members in-order to really make a difference. Project Seed has found a method of reaching out to families of their students that needs to be duplicated and implemented in schools all over this country. The program states, concerning family involvement: " Along with classroom instruction to students and professional development for teachers, Project Seed also seeks to involve the families of students in their academic success. In workshops designed for parents and families, Project Seed specialists share tips and strategies for working with students and mathematics topics for everyday life. Project Seed hosts events for families which celebrate the achievements of Seed students. At each school, Seed specialists attend parent-teacher meetings, school open houses, and offer services to the school to support existing family activities."

I believe Project Seed has opened the door to the many possibilities that exist in taking the necessary steps to improve the mathematical achievement and performance of African-American students. I am very much aware that each school, teacher and community has its own unique situations, circumstances and issues and some may be saying, "that sounds good, but it won't work at my school or with my teachers." Taking all of that into consideration, I strongly encourage us as educators, concerned parents and community members to research this program called Project Seed and whatever can be applied to our educational institutions or realities, let us be found doing so. The success that Project Seed has accomplished and is accomplishing needs to be replicated and duplicated when and wherever possible. Let us extract the many jewels that can be found in this program and integrate them into our realities as educators so that we can gain momentum and ground on our journey to improve our students educational experience.

I strongly believe we can accomplish this mighty task of raising the level of persistence, achievement and performance of Black students. All the pieces of the puzzle are present if we open our eyes. What we need is dedicated and devoted soldiers to place the pieces in their right place.

NOTES

NOTES

NOTES

NOTES

NOTES

NOTES

NOTES

NOTES